Ietsugu Ohara

Modern
Japanese Restaurant

images
Publishing

Published in Australia in 2015 by
The Images Publishing Group Pty Ltd
ABN 89 059 734 431
6 Bastow Place, Mulgrave, Victoria 3170, Australia
Tel: +61 3 9561 5544 Fax: +61 3 9561 4860
books@imagespublishing.com
www.imagespublishing.com

Copyright © The Images Publishing Group Pty Ltd 2015
The Images Publishing Group Reference Number: 1191

All rights reserved. Apart from any fair dealing for the purposes of private study, research, criticism or review as permitted under the Copyright Act, no part of this publication may be reproduced, stored in a retrieval system or transmitted in any form by any means, electronic, mechanical, photocopying, recording or otherwise, without the written permission of the publisher.

National Library of Australia Cataloguing-in-Publication entry

Title:	Modern Japanese Restaurant / Ietsugu Ohara (ed.).
ISBN:	9781864706352 (hardback)
Subjects:	Restaurants—Japan—Design and construction.
	Architecture—Japan—21st century.

Dewey Number: 725.710952

Coordinated and edited by Images Publishing, Shanghai office.

Printed by Toppan Leefung Printing (Shenzhen) Co. Ltd

IMAGES has included on its website a page for special notices in relation to this and our other publications. Please visit www.imagespublishing.com.

Every effort has been made to trace the original source of copyright material contained in this book. The publishers would be pleased to hear from copyright holders to rectify any errors or omissions.
The information and illustrations in this publication have been prepared and supplied by the contributor/s. While all reasonable efforts have been made to ensure accuracy, the publishers do not, under any circumstances, accept responsibility for errors, omissions and representations, express or implied.

MODERN RESTAURANTS AS THE LIFE PROPOSALS

Japanese restaurants are more than places for a full stomach.

As the Chinese saying goes, three generations of wealth cultivates good taste for food and clothes. A restaurant, shifting from a place to eat in the past to the space for a comfortable stay with distinguished taste and cultivation, requires long-term accumulation and appreciation of life, which makes people value the quality rather than the quantity of food. In this way, the space of a restaurant elevates from the level of materiality to spirituality, in which precise, acute, outstanding and in-depth design plays a crucial role.

The interior design of a Japanese restaurant which has been developed over a number of years makes people relate to the dining space naturally. As a matter of fact, in Japan, many practical factors attribute to people's attention to the restaurant design.

One of them is that people spend their increasing salary for food in Japan. Maybe due to the heavy pressure and the extra working hours, people find the immediate way of relaxing is to enjoy the dining time with friends or colleagues at a restaurant. Besides the cuisine, the fun of space is one of the other perks at the same time. The vast expense the Japanese spend on eating attributes to the fact that they comparably value more on the restaurant consumption, which drives the fierce competition among the restaurants. What makes the dining experience more impressive? The answer is design.

Every year many media and design organizations present awards to promote interior design of commercial space, particularly to the restaurant design. The design for restaurants extracts the tasty essence of delicate food, and extends it to the table, the interior, and even the landscape and gardens outside the window. Sometimes, the selection of a restaurant means to choose the customers sitting next to you who share the same taste in terms of food and space.

Japanese designers do well in combining the tradition with modernity, the inland with the overseas, the east with the west, nature with civilization; they are also skilled in editing and integration. Not only do they merge multiple factors into one, also they create a proper approach to display the unique mood, and bring up their own style through absorbing various aesthetics.

This book, *Modern Japanese Restaurant*, includes about fifty Japanese restaurant design projects, and elaborates them in five chapters: *Less is more*, drawing the outline of modern minimalism; *Crafts & Nostalgia*, the celebration of in-situ culture and local craftsmanship; *Theme restaurant*, bringing on exciting topics; *Outside the Box*, viewing the Japanese cuisine from different cultures; and *Modern Sparkles*, sharing the eureka moment of restaurant design. The content also covers all categories of Japanese food restaurant, ranging from ramen restaurant, sushi bars, and izayaka, etc. All these outstanding design cases would breakout the stereotypes, and stimulate more fun and imagination.

Restaurants are the part of modern life space; they are also the extension of lifestyles which open up new ways of life, and this is the future tendency of restaurant design. Restaurants could be considered as the starting point of new lifestyles, which derives from food, and extends to the notion for selecting food materials, utensils, furniture, green plants and tiny goods accompanied with the everyday life scenes. The modern restaurants allow more alterations and possibilities, different colors and varied aesthetics; also stimulate the excitement for adults who feel like entering an amusement park. Therefore, a successful restaurant design could provide inspiring sparkles, and triggers more possibilities.

After all, a restaurant serves as the place providing a wonderful dining experience. How the experience is extracted and stored are the challenges left for interior designers. A great memory about a restaurant is not limited within three dimensional spaces. The delicious food, the tableware connecting food and space, the art piece displayed or hanging on the wall, along with the considerate service, all these meticulous details designed will activate the senses of customers, who are able to enjoy the taste and space filled with aroma, with surprises and memorable moment. The design is far beyond itself, which takes the space as a carrier to make people happy, leaving them with a heart-felt and echoing aftertaste.

Tomic Wu / Wu Dung Lung, studied at the National Chiao Tung University. Wu holds a master degree in Industrial Design, and has published the book series *Design Tokyo* since 2006. He is a writer and designer, also involved in Exhibition design and book planning. Wu lectured for over hundreds of design symposium and other events. He is the founder and president of Tomic Design Atelier and Lianyun Underground. Website: www.tomicdesign.com

CONTENTS

LESS IS MORE

- 6 Shyo Ryu Ken, Kyobashi
- 10 IZAMA
- 16 Shun Shoku Lounge by Gurunavi
- 20 Cafe Coutume Aoyama
- 26 Snow Picnic
- 30 Helsinki Bakery
- 34 Cafeteria in Ushimado
- 38 Dream Dairy Farm Restaurant
- 42 Wine & Sweets Tsumons
- 48 Ceramika
- 54 Restaurant on the Sea
- 60 Salle de Sejour
- 64 Cafe in the Park

CRAFTS & NOSTALGIA

- 68 Sushi Marine
- 72 Shared Terrace
- 76 Itoman Gyomin Shokudo
- 80 Shubari
- 86 Izakaya Tsunagi
- 90 Cafe Kureon
- 94 Fukui, Bouyourou
- 98 Yoichi
- 102 Hana-Soba Yu
- 106 Starbucks Coffee at Dazaifu Tenmangu
- 110 Tsuruichi Yakiniku
- 116 Cha no Chimoto

OUTSIDE THE BOX

Ikibana Restaurant 120
Kaiseki Yoshiyuki & Horse's Mouth 126
HAMA 130
Uchi Lounge 136
Izakaya Kinoya 140
Musashi Izakaya Restaurant 144
Saboten, Beijing 150
Kemuri 156
Sushizilla 162
The Pasta & Grill's 168
BARBARESCO 172

THEME RESTAURANT

+green 176
Tokyo Baby Cafe 182
Cafe & Meal MUJI, Chengdu 186
Kotokoto Dining 190
Cafe Ki 196
Restaurant Izaki 200
Secession 204
Bluberi Stonebridge 208
Lani Yogurt 210
Chowa 212

MODERN SPARKLE

Teeq 218
Aluminum Flower Garden 222
Abenoma 224
Cafe/Day 226
Saboten, Hong Kong 230
L'angolino 236
Yoshi Bar 2nd 240
Nautilus 242
Tokyo Kushi Bar 246
Sushi Tsujita 248

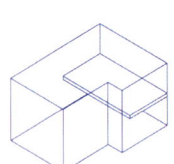 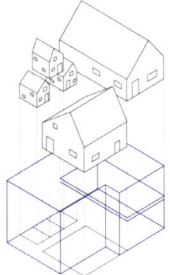 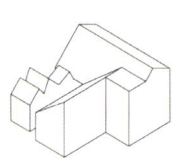 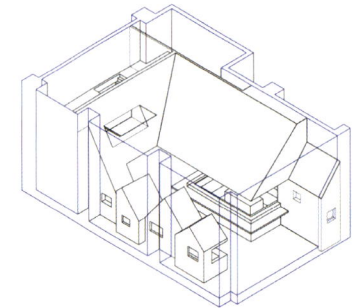 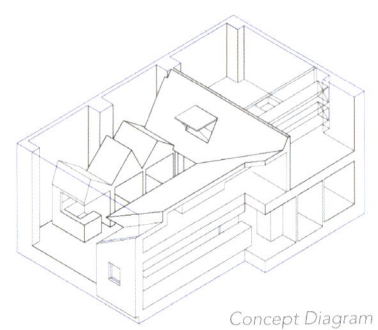

Concept Diagram

Shyo Ryu Ken, Kyobashi

DESIGNER Ietsugu Ohara / STILE   **USE** Restaurant   **LOCATION** Kyobashi, Osaka, Japan   **AREA** 122.67m²   **PHOTOGRAPHER** Hirokazu Matsuoka

This is a new branch of the local famous Japanese noodle restaurant, Shyo Ryu Ken at Kyobashi, Osaka, which is built under a railroad overpass.

There is a business district and downtown area around this place. The theme of this shop is to provide a gathering place for the local community. That is why its appearance is open to the sideway, not like traditional closed structure. There are some building codes on the under a railroad overpass constructions, therefore all the other shops tend to look similar. The designer wanted to defy the stereotype and tried to pursue the new-look at this limited environment. The challenge was to create the original structure under that condition.

Inspired by Nagaya (a traditional Japanese tenement house) style, there are different shapes of triangle roofs inside the shop and each table under the roof looks like a dining room for each customer, yet one side of the each cell is wide open to the center of the shop and it connects customer with friendly staff, cooks in the kitchen and other customers.

To create an open structure and to pursue the new-look at this limited environment, the designer assumed the post and beam of overpass as the base of its mockup after struggling with the traditional way of construction which makes a spatially-closed place along with walls and ceiling. In this way, the designer could expand the inside-out image and built the shop synchronizes with this street.

The designer used steel doors and hardened glass walls as its exterior and decorated it only with the shop logo in a simple but beautiful way. There are different shapes of triangle roofs inside and each area under the roof is like a dining room for each customer. Yet one side of the cell is opened to connect with the entire space and furthermore, with the community. Utilizing Japanese traditional (and reasonable) materials, the designer created the non-traditional simple, but beautiful structure.

Materials
exterior wall   hardened glass and steel door;
interior   wooden framework, ply board and plastering materials to finish.

01. General view from the facade
02. The open kitchen interacts with the dining room.
03. View toward "nagaya" from the entrance hall

04. Detail view of "nagaya"
05. Aerial view of the hall
06. View towards "nagaya" from the big table

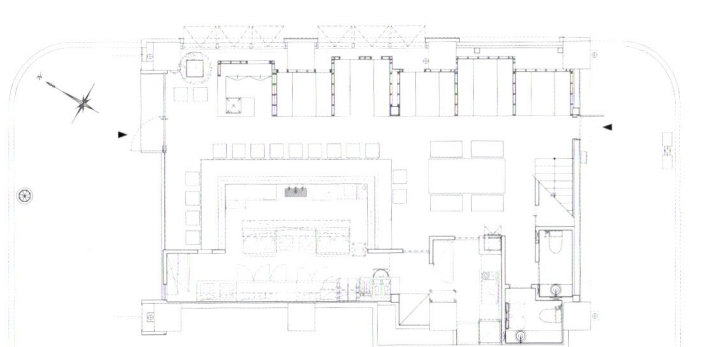
First Floor Plan

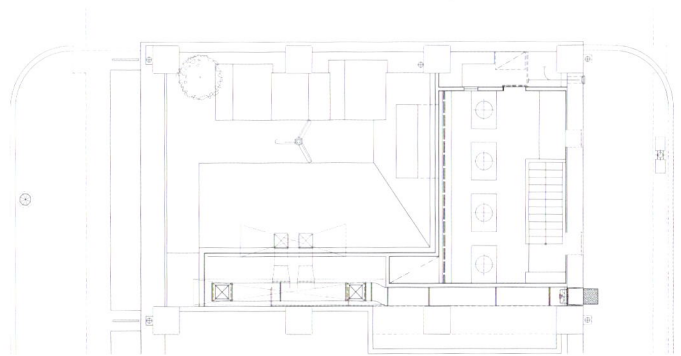
Second Floor Plan

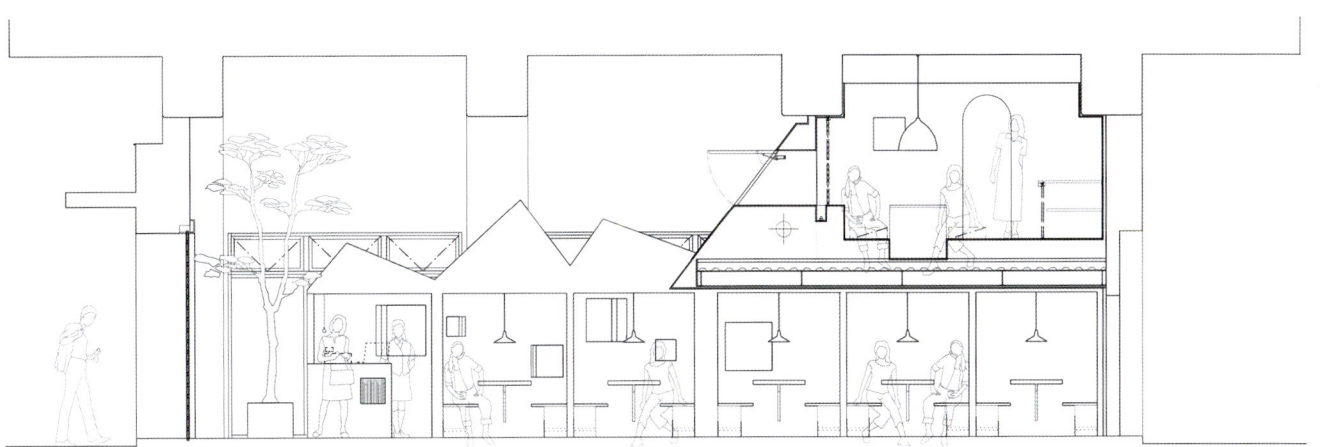
Sketch

IZAMA

DESIGNER Yuko Nagayama & Associates **USE** Restaurant **LOCATION** Kyoto, Japan
PHOTOGRAPHER Nobutada Omote

Located on a center of Kyoto, along the historical street of Nakagyo-ku there lies a one-storied Japanese restaurant "IZAMA" which is constructed of two parts, a cozy traditional warehouse and a large corner cut from a recently built hotel. The interior of the hotel is partitioned with two kinds of curtains, one is that of stainless steel copy of the Japanese bamboo screen and the other is that of arch-shape iron plate (4.5mm thickness) of which two surfaces are covered by Japanese white stucco (1.5mm thickness), which recalls the white wall of the traditional warehouse, the former partitions dining tables lightly with a transmissivity suitable for the restaurant and the letter partitions the interior the interior to make a few small spaces used for dining rooms. The iron plate was weight-saved mechanically and visually: namely iron plates were blanked with many disks as mechanical strength was less demanded for the arch-shape curtain and covered by with color producing a lightness perception like white paper. The stucco covered iron plate has 8mm thickness and shapely cuts various spaces, the garden and dining rooms, as ultimately thin partition walls.

The large table in the central room emits candle-like dim light owing to the special paint that kneaded with brass powder. In the morning breakfast buffets are displayed on the tables. The central illumination is set to a suitable height to separate people lining up in the buffet and those sitting in the opposite side. The inside wall of the warehouse is finished by the Japanese black stucco and the warehouse ceiling hangs 64 ceiling lights that are reflected by the black table underneath. Pitch-black darkness spreads in the upper garret behind the ceiling light. The designer tried to vitalize a simple-designed construction with the play of light reflected from surfaces of constituent materials. In the end the interior changes the atmosphere from time to time the depending upon external light.

01. Looking at the courtyard over an 8mm Japanese stucco wall from the inside
02. The front entrance
03. The interior framed by a 8mm Japanese stucco wall
04. Interior details
05. An original porcelain shade and a screen curtain of the stainless steel mesh.

06-08. Interior views

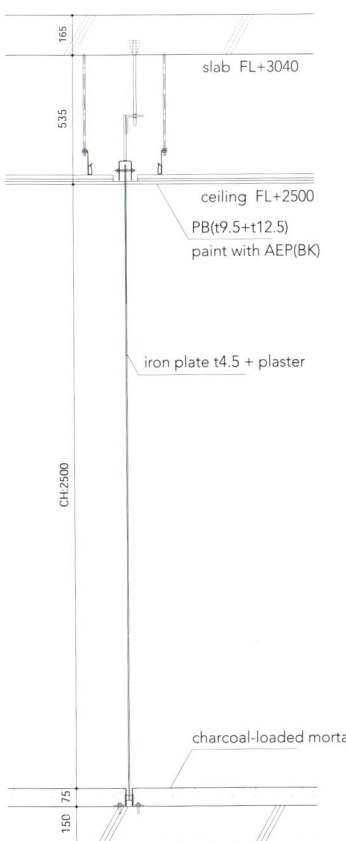

Hanging Wall Plan

① Shimachi Street Side Entrance
② Lobby Side Entrance
③ Cashier Counter
④ Existing Warehouse
⑤ Pantry
⑥ Kitchen

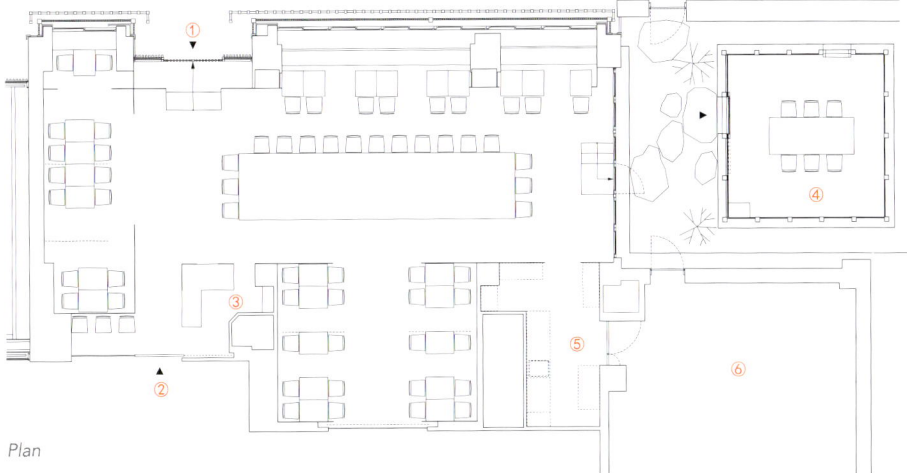

Plan

09. Interior details
10. The reception of the restaurant
11. The entrance of the traditional warehouse
12. The central room with a large table

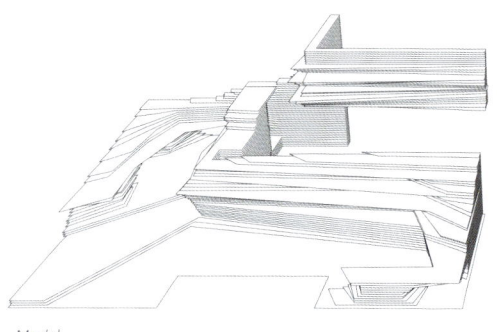

Model

Shun Shoku Lounge by Gurunavi

DESIGNER Kengo Kuma & Associates **USE** Bar / Lounge **LOCATION** Osaka, Japan **AREA** 84m²
PHOTOS Kengo Kuma & Associates

The designer piled up pieces of wooden panels to build the interior like topography. Various food-related items are laid out on this wooden ground. We expected that the chemistry would be just right for eating and the wooden stratum. Layered configuration has also been designed for V&A at Dundee. This lounge is in a way like a nesting inside V&A.

01-02. Facade
03-04. Interior overview

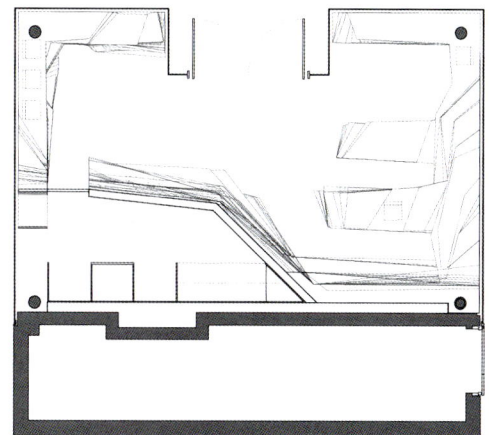
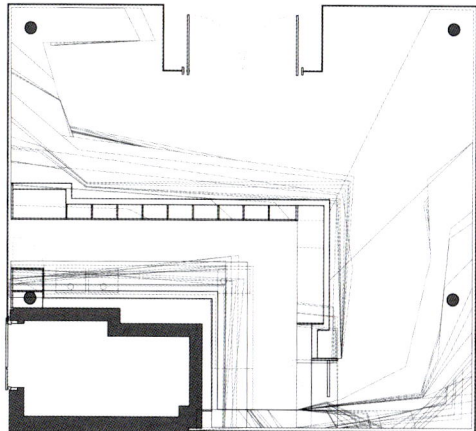

Plan

05-06. Interior details
07-08. Interior overview

Cafe Coutume Aoyama

DESIGNER CUT architectures **USE** Cafe **LOCATION** Tokyo, Japan **AREA** 85m² **CLIENT** Baycrews Coutume Div. **PHOTOGRAPHER** David Foessel

Following the flagship cafe Coutume rue de Babylone in Paris which opened in 2011 and the coffee cart within the Finnish Institute in Paris which opened in 2013 both designed by CUT architectures, we've been invited to develop the first cafe Coutume abroad, in the heart of Tokyo in the Aoyama district. Our aim was to keep the strong identity we created for the Coutume brand while adapting it to the Tokyo location. At the crossing between a Parisian coffee shop and a laboratory, Cafe Coutume Aoyama offers a two sided space.

On the entrance side the laboratory is set up under a white hygienic grid ceiling with integrated LED panels lighting up the bar. The bar and cashier is composed of two tiled blocks referring to the chemistry boards. On the other side, the seating area is set under the hollow version of the bar ceiling: white lacquered frames in continuity with the ceiling grid of the laboratory area. The entire flooring is made out of oak parquetry using different layouts: Chantilly layout in front of the bar, Hungarian layout on the way to the restrooms, traditional layout for the seating area. A single tile is integrated within the parquetry in front of the bar, echoing with the treatment of the custom-made tables of the seating area. The wall base of the interior walls as well as on the exterior facade is clad with white tiles up to 1m creating a continuous line surrounding the entire space both inside and outside.

On the street side another block made of tiles and glass is hosting a roasting sampler, high stools and small Japanese plants. Behind the bar, a translucent glazed wall hiding the kitchen integrates glass shelves for display. In the back, a large communal table with a large planter offers ten seats under an illuminated printed glass volume. Following the ceiling grid the hanging lights are made out of ceramic lamp holders and Japanese tubular bulbs. One the surrounding walls vintage French ceramic bathroom fixtures are combined with oak sticks to create coat hangers and holders for the mobile lamps used by the workers during the construction of the cafe.

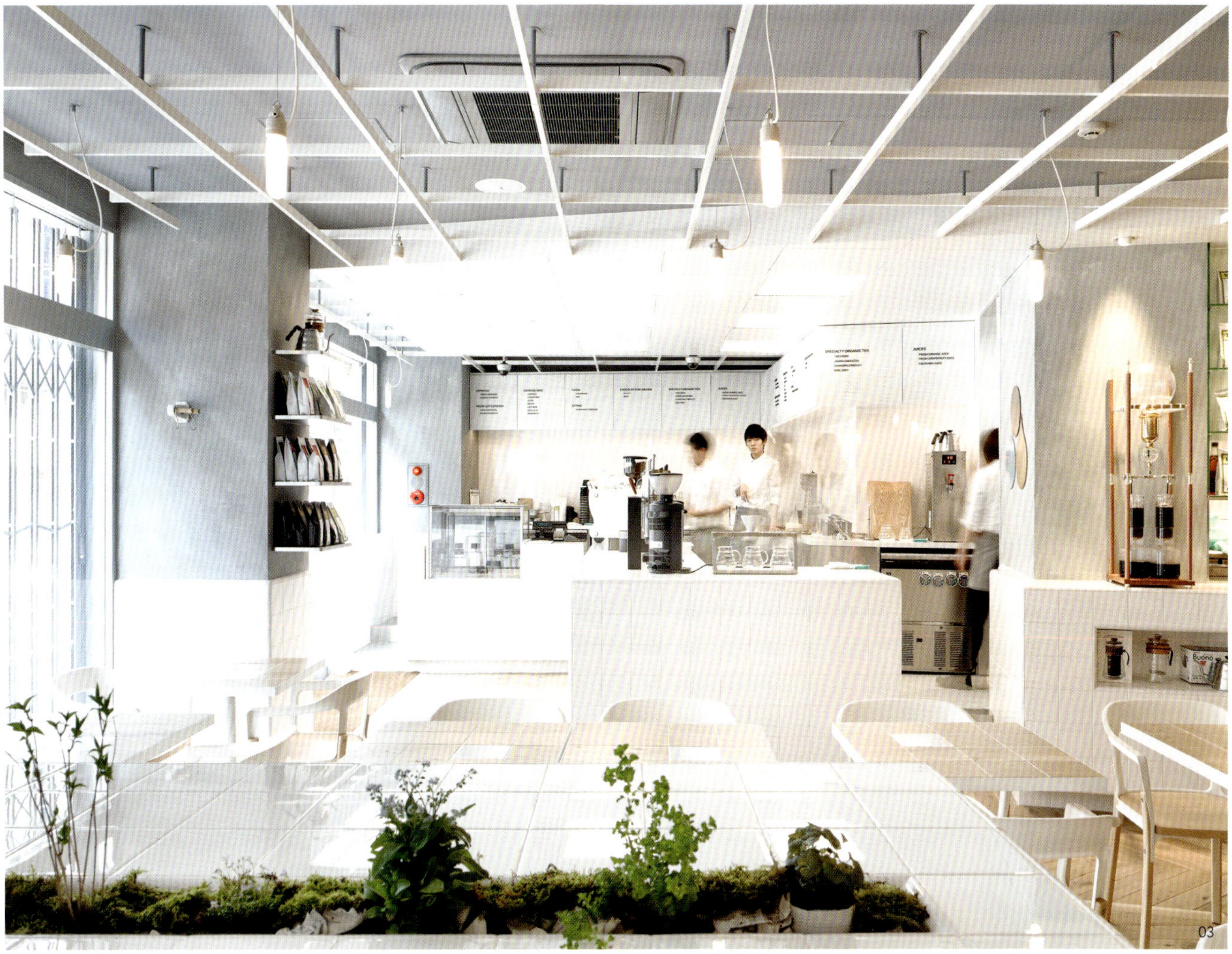
03

ESPRESSO
SINGLE ESPRESSO
DOUBLE ESPRESSO
MICRO-LOT ESPRESSO
SINGLE ESPRESSO
DOUBLE ESPRESSO
ESPRESSO BASE
CORTADO
CAPPUCCINO
LATTE
MOCHA
CAFÉ NOIR
ICED LATTE
SHAKERATO
FILTER
STEAMPUNK
V60
EXTRAS
EXTRA SHOT ESPRESSO
04

05

06

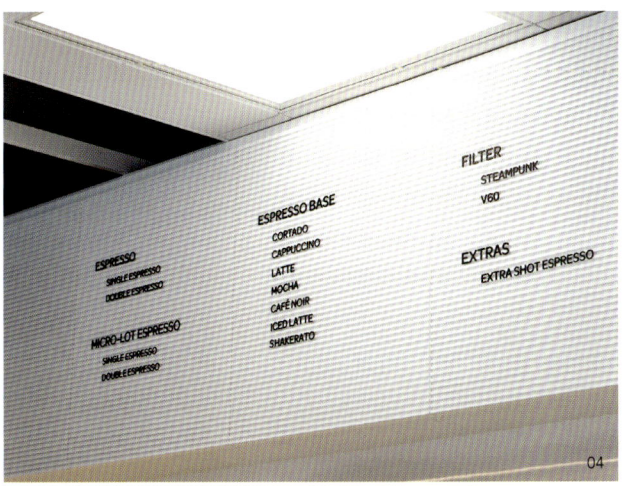

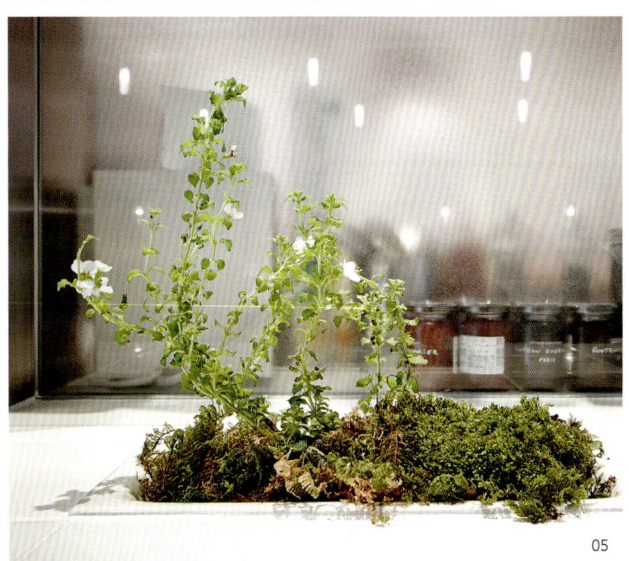

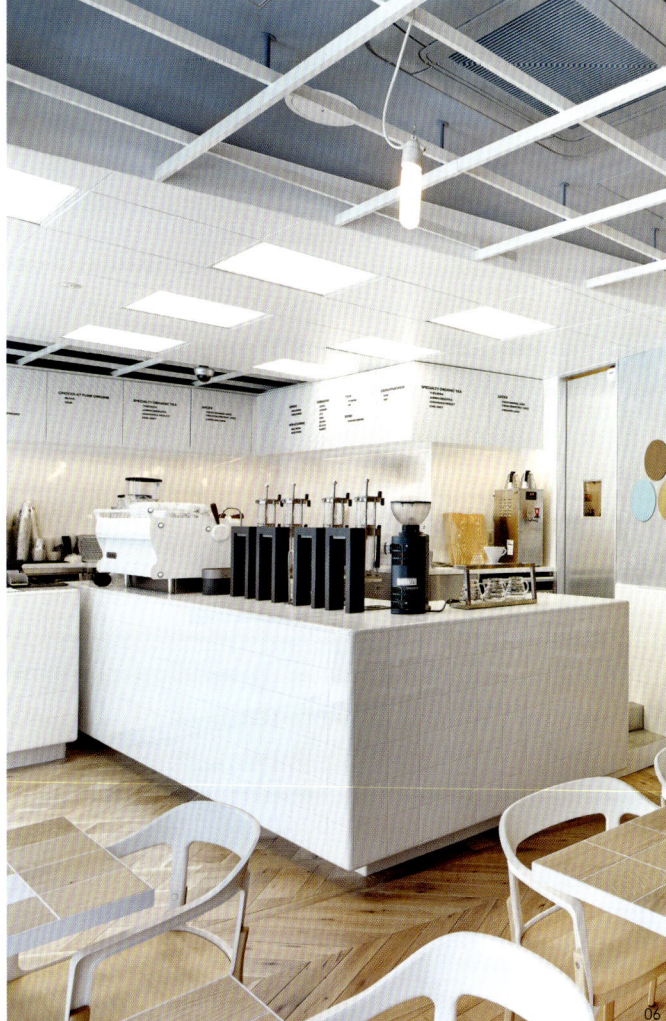

Street Facade

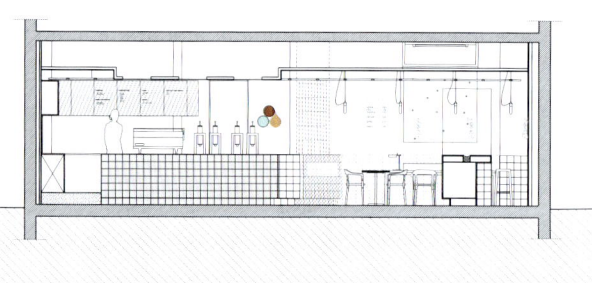

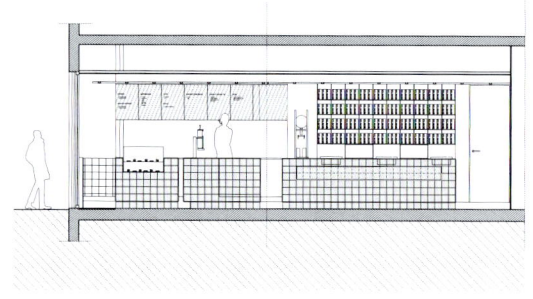

Section

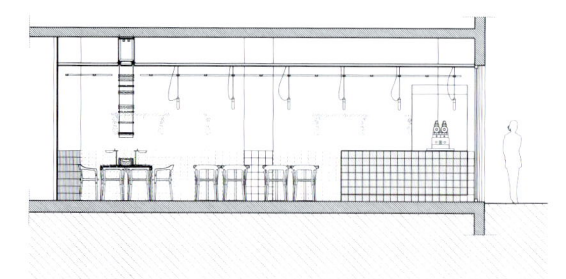

01. Interior
02. Facade
03. Interior
04-06. Interior details
07-09. Interior

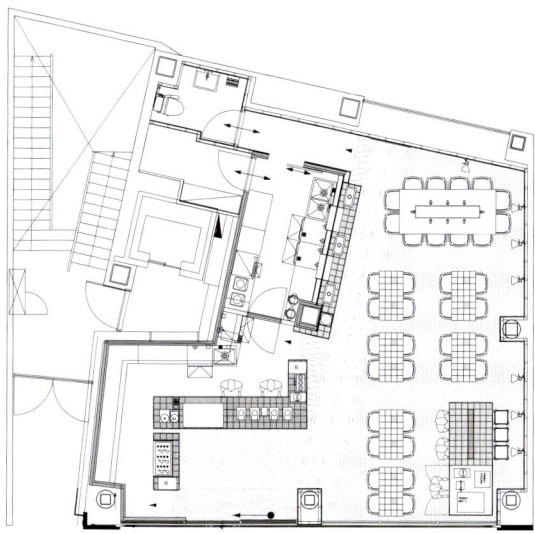

Upper Floor Plan

10-14. Interior details

Snow Picnic

DESIGNER TORAFU ARCHITECTS **USE** Cafe / Shop **LOCATION** Tokyo, Japan **AREA** 64.14m²
PHOTOGRAPHER Takumi Ota

We performed the interior and exterior design for a gelato store that opened in a shopping street of Nakano, Tokyo, where customers can enjoy watching their order being prepared on the spot through a performance whereby liquid nitrogen is mixed into a liquid concentrate of ice cream to produce gelato.

The entrance features a glass facade stretching the whole frontage facing the street while the floor layout features three landings of different heights that lead to the highest point at the back of the shop. Here can be found the preparation counter that acts as a kitchen and a stage for the performance which can be seen from the street and whereby smoke is produced by using liquid nitrogen.

By varying the floor finishing in each area using flooring, linoleum and vintage tiles that extend all the way to the street, we were able to turn one small space into three distinct ones. Moreover, by using chairs of different sizes, it is possible to sit all around the table straddling these different areas in the middle of the store. Customers can also choose their favorite spot from cantilever tables seating and a sofa placed next to the glass entrance.

Furthermore, the bright tones of the store's interior contrasting with the toilet and back store areas painted in black, the table in the middle that features the same tile finishing of the floor in the front, the existing wooden columns mended using wooden plugs, and the soft-tones on the walls switching at an angle like sunlight entering from above, etc., are all designed to strike a balance between new and old materials and colors alike.

We sought to create a cozy and inviting lounge filled with plants that will serve as a showcase for the store's unique gelato preparation method, while presenting the aspect of a laboratory with white smoke spilling from the black counter.

01. Interior overview
02. Counter
03-04. Interior

05-08. Interior details

Helsinki Bakery

DESIGNER Studio Arihiro Miyake   **USE** Restaurant / Cafe / Bakery   **LOCATION** Osaka, Japan
PHOTOGRAPHER Nomurakougei Co.,Ltd

The main concept of this restaurant is simple and modern interpretation of Finish fork-style. The space is composited dynamically with over 7m bar counter, long table and full glass showcase, yet natural wooden and white colour gives warm and clean impression. The wooden patch-work like facade is designed after Finish classic fork house covered with layers of birch plate. The furniture and their layout is the image of birch forest, and there is a motif of birch leaves drown on the walls which only visible by lighting angles. The suspension lamps are originally designed to create the leaking light of wooden house.

It functions as the restaurant – cafe and also take-out bakery. The key idea for service is natural and health food, all dishes are Scandinavian traditional recipes and bread is made of rye wheat.

01. Entrance
02. Facade
03. Original suspension lamp for main table
04. Original floor lamp for entrance
05. Restaurant interior

06-07. Restaurant interior
08. Bakery area
09. Suspension lamp detail
10. Bakery showcase

① Kitchen for Food
② Kitchen for Baking
③ Bar Counter
④ Main Table
⑤ Bakery Showcase
⑥ Bakery Shelves

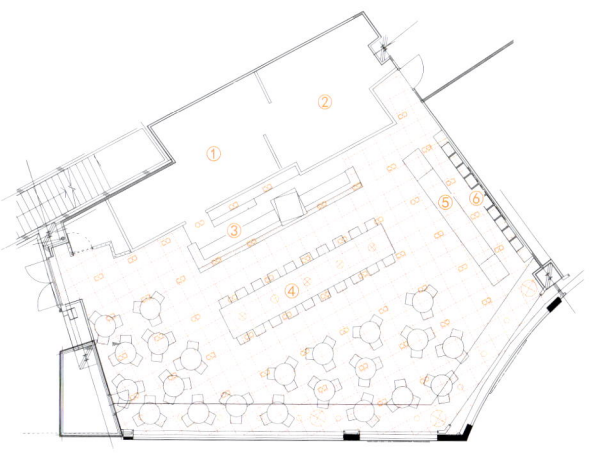

Plan

① Kitchen
② Cafeteria
③ Lounge

Wooden Framework Model

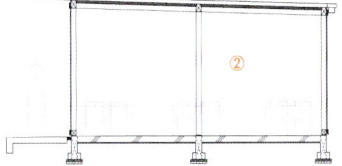

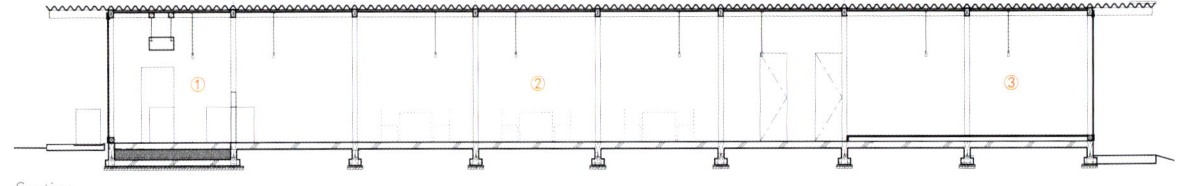

Section

Cafeteria in Ushimado

DESIGNER Niji Architects, AI Design   **USE** Cafe / Shop   **LOCATION** Okayama, Japan   **AREA** 166.32m²   **PHOTOS** Niji Architects

This cafeteria is a timber framed, single-story building located in Ushimado of Setouchi city, Okayama prefecture, Japan. It serves as a canteen for a local construction company as well as a cafeteria for the local community.

The building structure and its finishes are kept simple and the presence of the building is kept to a bare minimum. The building design focuses mainly on its primary function as a cafeteria for the local people and to familiarize itself to the community.

The folded metal plate roof is directly fixed to the 3m grid timber structural frame, which consists of 120mmx120mm timber used for columns, foundation, bracings and 180mmx120mm timber beams. The building completes itself with glass walls, which are fixed directly to the timber structure with timber battens.

The detailing and materials intentionally designed to appear unrefined to create a relaxing atmosphere helping visitors to unwind within the space. With a single large internal space and full aperture to the external views, this highly transparent building becomes a bright, open and inviting cafeteria.

We believe this construction method can also be used for other building types. It can be a prototype of new prefabricated timber construction with endless possibilities for further development.

MATERIALS
structure   *exposed timber;*
roof   *folded metal;*
external facade   *clear float glass (t=10mm) with glass film;*
window   *wooden sash and aluminum sash*

01. Inside details
02. Exterior
03. A folded metal plate roof is directly fixed to the structural timber frame.
04. The column, beam and brace
05. Passage

06

① Kitchen
② Cafeteria
③ Lounge

Plan

07

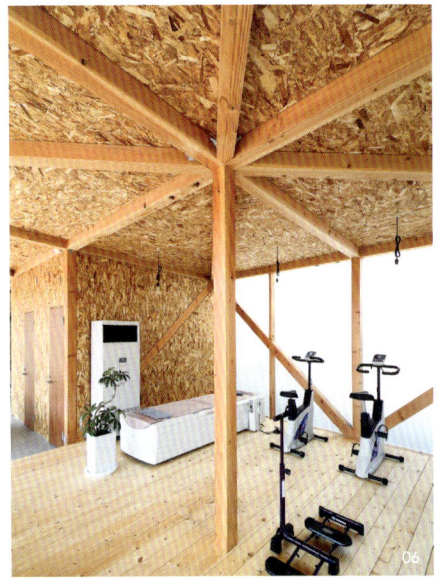

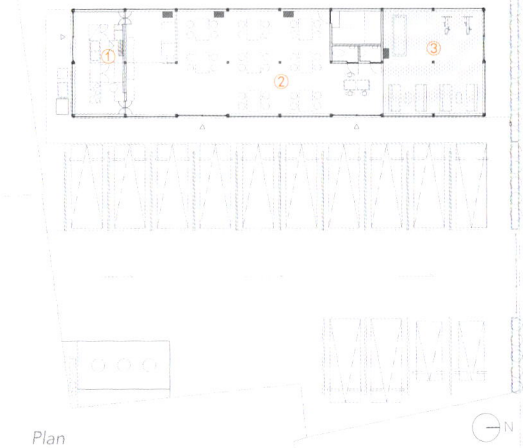

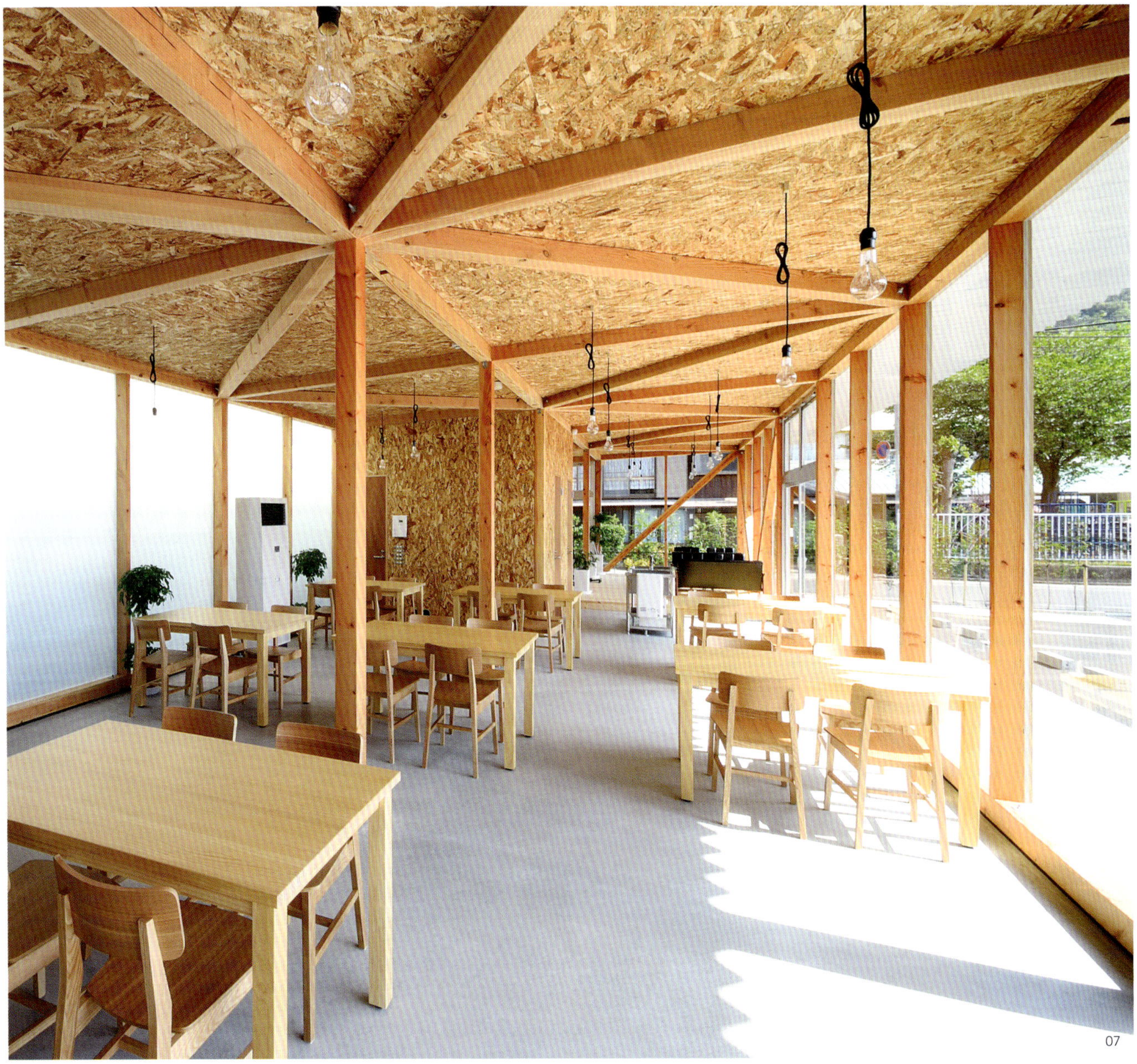

06. The small space is provided for working out.
07. The daytime interior and the view of the open-plan cafeteria
08. The evening view of the cafe
09. The night lighting

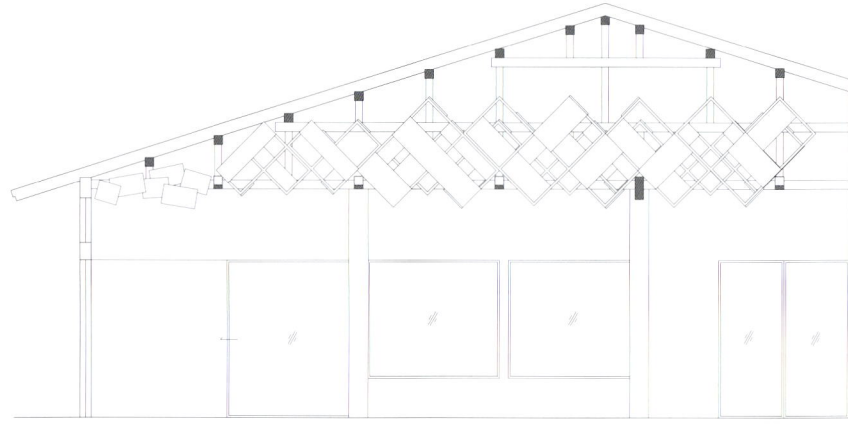
Section

Dream Dairy Farm Restaurant

DESIGNER Moriyuki Ochiai Architects **USE** Restaurant **LOCATION** Chiba, Japan **AREA** 75m²
CLIENT Dream Dairy Farm **CONSTRUCTOR** Aslego **PHOTOGRAPHER** Atsushi Ishida

The following interior design was realized for a restaurant built on a farm surrounded by a lush forest.

Since the menu is characterized by the fact that dairy products, such as cheese and yogurt, made from fresh milk produced on-site at the dairy farm is used in each and all of their dishes, we were tasked with providing a space to attractively showcase said menu by evoking the imagery associated with the power of fresh ingredients and the natural setting of the forest surrounding the farm on which these quality products are made throughout the entire space.

The three-dimensional white lattice nesting above the beams of the existing wooden structure forms the canopy of a forest that brings together the old and the contemporary by suggesting the superimposition of time and space.

Since the ceiling is composed of a volume peering through a larger wooden frame, layers of glossy translucent resin boards were fitted on certain surfaces to produce a luminous body providing subdued lighting to the entire space. This layered structure will be perceived differently depending on the diners' relative position and line of sight at any given time. Moreover, the light reflected off and penetrating the resin boards all come together to produce intricate and constantly evolving expressions.

As the light from one structure beckons and resonates with the light from the next, individual shards of light gather into sheaves of light that dart through the space, or into splashes of light that escape onto the dining area gushing like the flow of a river. Whether this transmutation of light occurs in a dynamic or subtle manner, the resulting expressions offer an ever-changing shower of light that can be fully experienced depending on where one is standing and looking to.

By applying a special paint echoing the texture of plain soil found on the farm to the walls of the restaurant and matching these with the natural warmth of timber, we aimed to create a warm and intimate atmosphere. Interestingly, the shape of pendant lighting hanging at regular intervals appear to depict drops of cheese and yogurt dripping from the canopy while imparting a light rhythm to the space. While the rough grain motif of the counter can be interpreted as a thundering waterfall, the columns' wooden accents conferred by a special paint lend the space the energy of living trees.

By superimposing time and space and bridging the old and the new, the repeated entwinement of lattice and light offers a mystic illumination and the spatial experience of penetrating into a deep forest. Thus, we have created a space in which the restaurant's patrons can enjoy a meal made using fresh dairy products while being immersed in an atmosphere brimming with the vitality of a forest of vibrant light and lattice.

MATERIALS
ceiling timber, resin boards, painted board
floor wood
wall special painted drywall, wood

01. Full view (from outside)
02. Full view (reflection on the glass)
03. Detail of Lattice

04-07. Full view

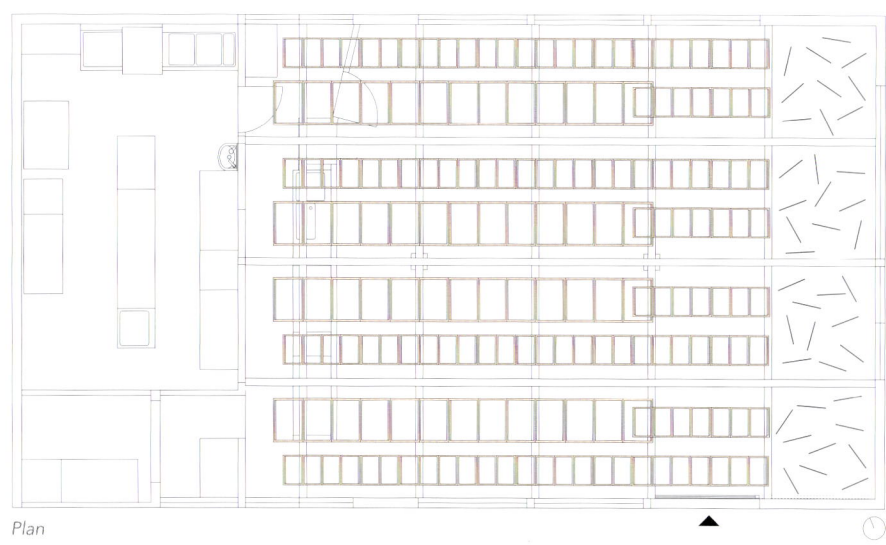

Plan

Wine & Sweets Tsumons

DESIGNER Koichi Futatusmata, Tomoki Katada / CASE-REAL   **USE** Bar/Shop   **LOCATION** Fukuoka, Japan   **CLIENT** WINE & SWEETS TSUMONS   **AREA** 65.3m²   **PHOTOGRAPHER** Hiroshi Mizusaki

This is a design for both shop and bar with an original concept to provide a new combination of western confectionery and wine.

The site is located in the central part of Fukuoka city and is surrounded by the sprawl of densely-packed residential and mid-rise buildings. The small site is dominated by multi-storey apartments. However, it is the owner's earnest desire to build a one-storey building.

The owner is both patissier and sommelier. As a result of many meetings with her, we decided to create architecture as if it presented her character as an artisan. In other words, we aimed at providing architecture which has an earnest and dignified sight contracting with the bustle of the city. Additionally, we are making a conscious decision to build a one-story "oasis" against the city "jungle" with its multi-storey buildings.

The building incorporates a pent broadly sloped southward in a box-shaped volume. The retail space is located on the road side and the counter space is in the rear. The courtyard is located on the south side facing these spaces and being as a staff workflow line. These space compositions allow the shop to retain a calm atmosphere, contrasting with the busy street. Additionally, the background of both main spaces becomes an annex letting mild light in. The horizontal continuous windows to trim the view are designed outside the fire spread line, which enable these windows to be wire-free regarding regulations. Consequently, a clear view of surroundings was retained.

The finish used in the courtyard includes large-fruit asphalt single materials continuing to the roof. These materials can store water, so plants such as small ivy, which are planted on the wall, will build up gradually in the uneven wall and roof surface. The roof will eventually become another "facade" and it will have a presence of a "spot garden" for the people who live in the neighborhood.

The upper space, Sky, which is created by the relationship between the one-storey building and the surrounding buildings, is to be one of the features of the building. This character allows the shop itself to exude its meaning and the building which is mixed with the cityscape is expected to improve the locality's atmosphere together with the region.

01. Interior view of the counter space
02. Front view of the facade
03. View of the courtyard
04. Ivy planted on the wall of courtyard

Drawing

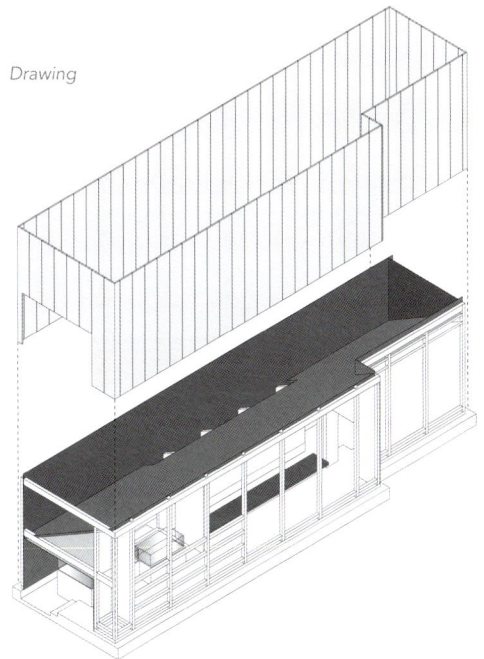

05

06

05. Continuous view of the counter, kitchen, and courtyard
06. Interior view of the counter space
07. View of the counter space and the partition made of terrazzo
08. Wine and sweets displayed in shop space
09. Interior view of the shop space

10-11. Counter chair designed by Futatsumata for this project
12. Night view of the counter space
13. General night view of the interior
14. Night view

① Shop
② Bar Counter
③ Passage
④ Courtyard
⑤ Kitchen
⑥ Toilet

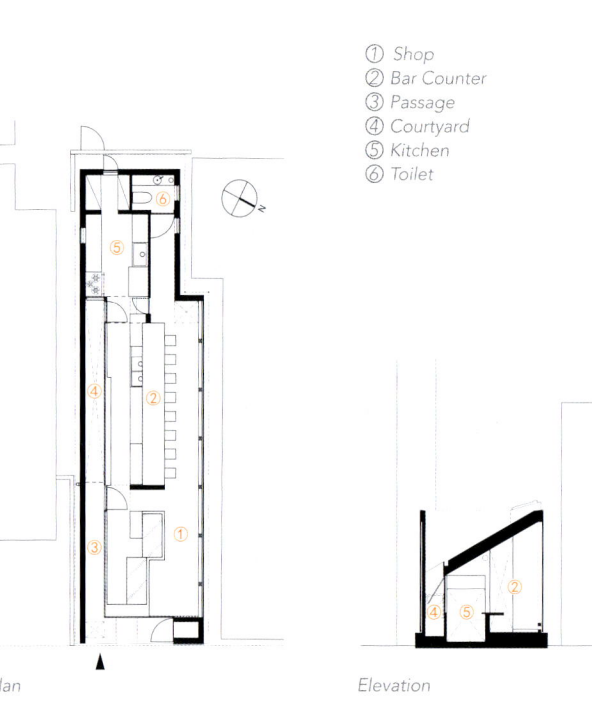

Plan   Elevation

Ceramika

DESIGNER Claesson Koivisto Rune Architects **USE** Cafe / Showroom **LOCATION** Matsumoto, Japan
CLIENT Ceramika **PHOTOGRAPHER** Takumi Ota

The Ceramika showroom is located in Matsumoto, which is in the mountainous Nagano Prefecture, 200km away on northwest of Tokyo. Matsumoto is such a big city but it is a centre of traditional crafts, such as wood, lacquerware and fabric. The cups and plates and bowls at Ceramika are European instead of Japanese. But this is what modern Japan is about: opened up to the world while never deviating from the strong Japaneses heritage of aesthetics and quality.

In line with these principles, one may assume, was the commission to design the Ceramika flagship store given to the Swedish architects Claesson Koivisto Rune – undeniably Scandinavians, but well accustomed to Japan. Ceramika is represented with shops in every major city throughout Japan and through mail order and online business, while Matsumoto is the home town.

The Ceramika showroom is located in the city centre in a former city hall building along the Matsumoto River. The space was completely stripped and the new interior is deliberately simple, at the same time, with meticulously refined details. The layout is on a strict repetitive grid. The colors and materials of the interior were chosen to harmonize with the porcelain which is mostly blue and white. A small cafe is situated both indoors and outdoors. The aim was to create a space which was strict, yet humble.

The wood furniture was designed by Claesson Koivisto Rune and manufactured by carpenter master Hara-san. This made it possible to use smaller proportions and have a much higher degree of refinement, than usually in a project like this.

Many of the pieces in the project was designed especially by Claesson Koivisto Rune and manufactured locally in Japan. Such as the display furniture, tables and clothes hangers. Other pieces also designed by Claesson Koivisto Rune were produced by manufacturers such as Almedahls, David design, Tacchini, and Wästberg.

The project was a fruitful collaboration between the architect and the client. The client and owner of the Ceramika showroom, Mr. Hiroshi Arai, took a personal pride in attending to the quality and execution of every detail in the project.

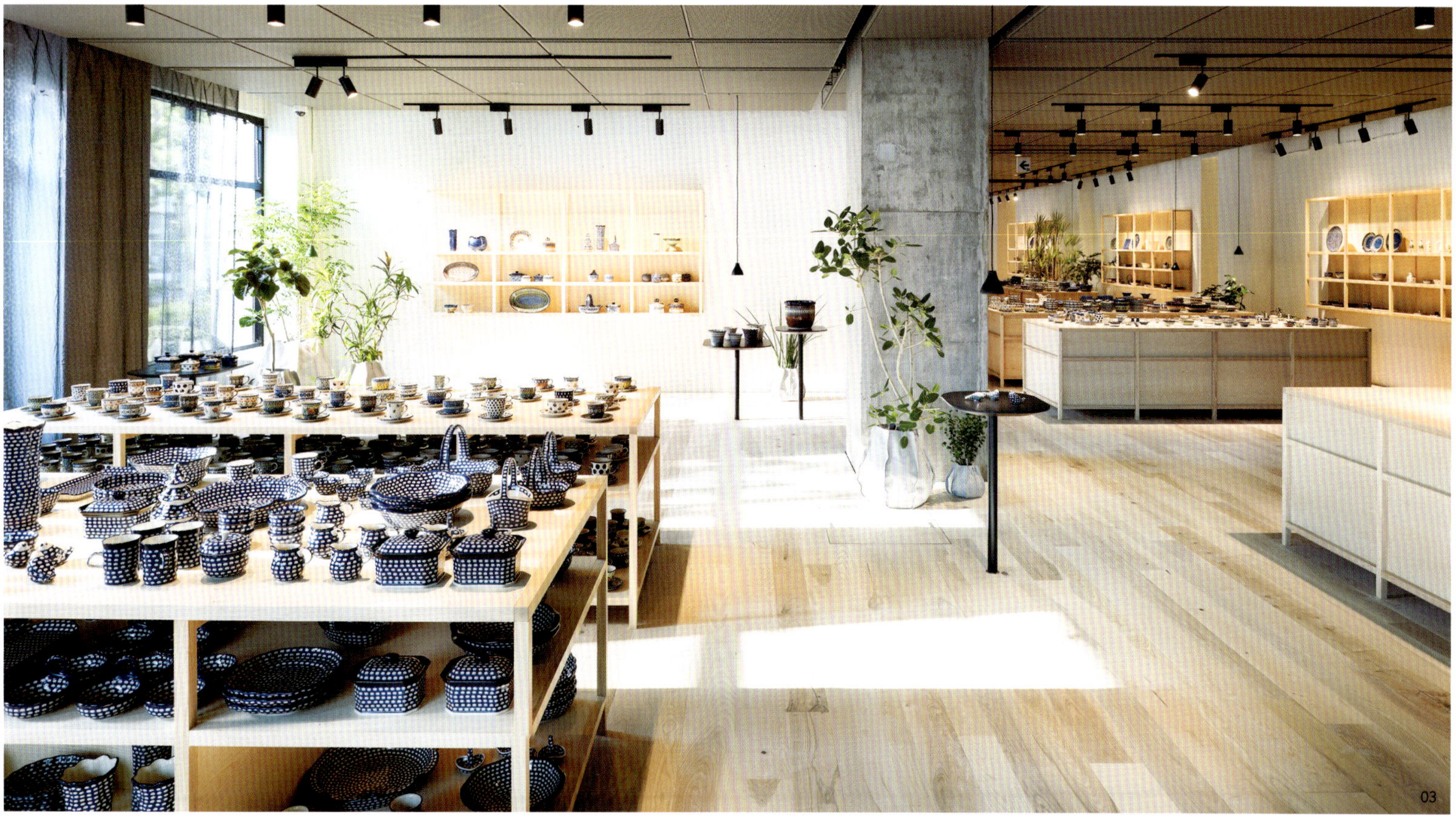

03

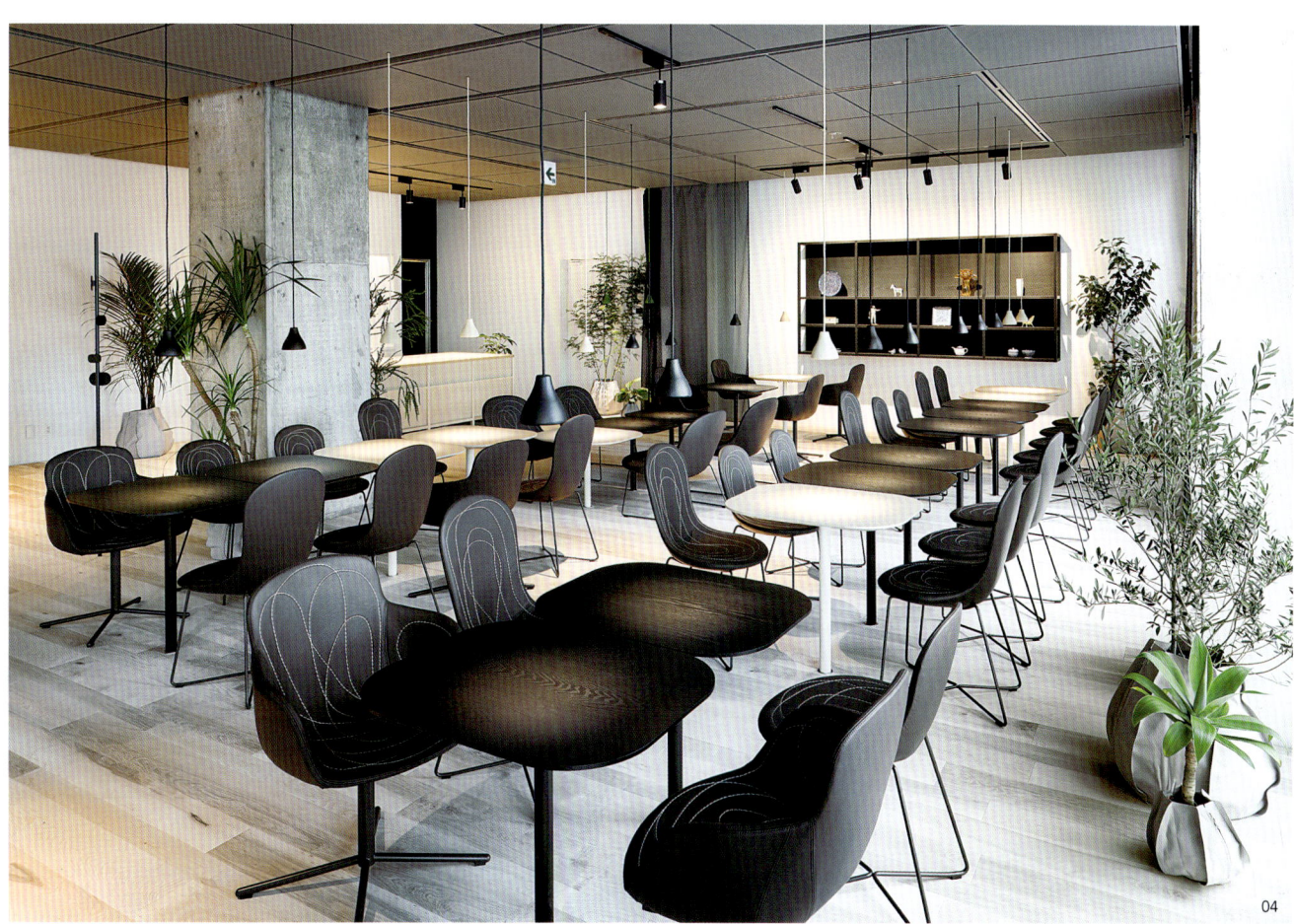

01. Cafe area
02. Facade
03. Showroom Interior
04. Cafe area

04

05-07. Interior area
08-09. Ceramic on display
10-11. Cafe seat area

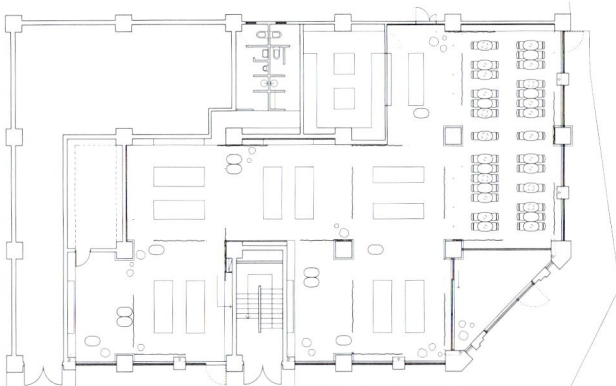

Plan

08-09. Ceramic on display
10-11. Cafe seat area

Restaurant on the Sea

DESIGNER Koichi Futatusmata, Yasushi Arikawa / CASE-REAL   **USE** Restaurant   **LOCATION** Kagawa, Japan   **CLIENT** Circle House Cooperation   **AREA** 471m²   **PHOTOGRAPHER** Hiroshi Mizusaki

This design project is for a restaurant atop Teshima, one of the islands floating in the Seto Inland Sea.
As one of the venues for the Setouchi Triennale which was hosting its 2nd edition in 2013, Teshima has been a place where dairy and rice cropping were active for decades.

Due to depopulation the traditional rice terraces were once desolated, though gradually recovering its richness by the help of many volunteers.
With such backgrounds, the main objective of this restaurant is to provide a "Place for Food", not only for the visitors from all over the world who come for art, but also for the local islanders. Fitted with a public kitchen to be made available to a variety of people directly in front of the building's main approach, the rich communication built surrounding food will emerge. It was with this vision of such a new island culture being nurtured that the building was designed.
This duo-arch structure running along the coast, totaling to 40m in length, has most of its interior and exterior walls, and roofs covered with light wave plates, also with a large portion of its sea-facing side open as a terrace. This terrace captures the breathtaking views of the ocean extending forth, but also becomes an important element of this design as a hub through which all features, such as the kitchen, restaurant and public kitchen, are all connected, both in physicality and in consciousness. The terrace portion of the roof uses a light wave plate with a permeability that conjures a feeling of openness, and natural sunlight pouring through the roofs of both arches creates differing atmospheres in the indoor and outdoor spaces. Additionally, the foundation of the building, raised as a measure against the flood of tidal waves, uses a red-brown concrete, as if the earth itself had been raised, providing a contrast to the presence of the blue sky and ocean continuing beyond. It was our aim to provide architecture that coexists with the island, accepting both the overwhelming blessings and ferocity of nature in Setouchi.

01. Ocean view from the terrace
02. Exterior view from the ocean
03. Ocean view from the sink area
04. Exterior view of entrance
05. View of the terrace

06. View of the terrace
07. Interior view of the restaurant
08. View of the terrace

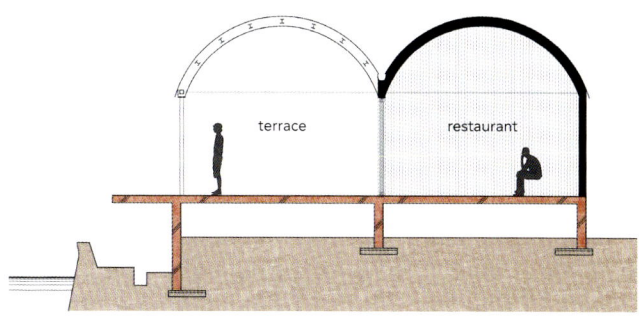

Section

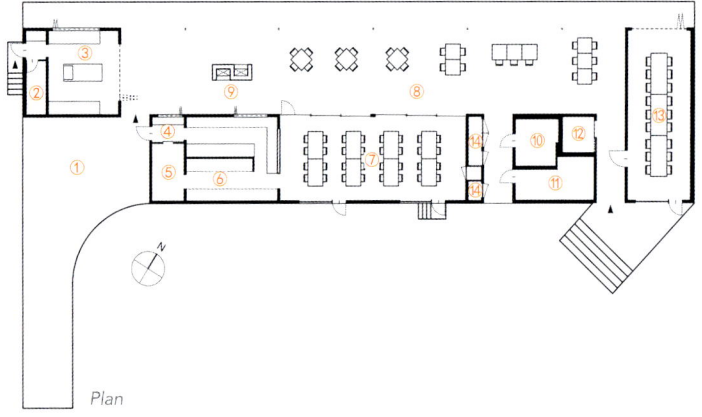

Plan

① Entrance
② Food Stock
③ Public Kitchen
④ Reception Desk
⑤ Staff Room
⑥ Kitchen
⑦ Restaurant
⑧ Terrace
⑨ Sink Area
⑩ Men's Toilet
⑪ Lady's Toilet
⑫ Multipurpose Toilet
⑬ Private Room
⑭ Stock Room

09

10

11

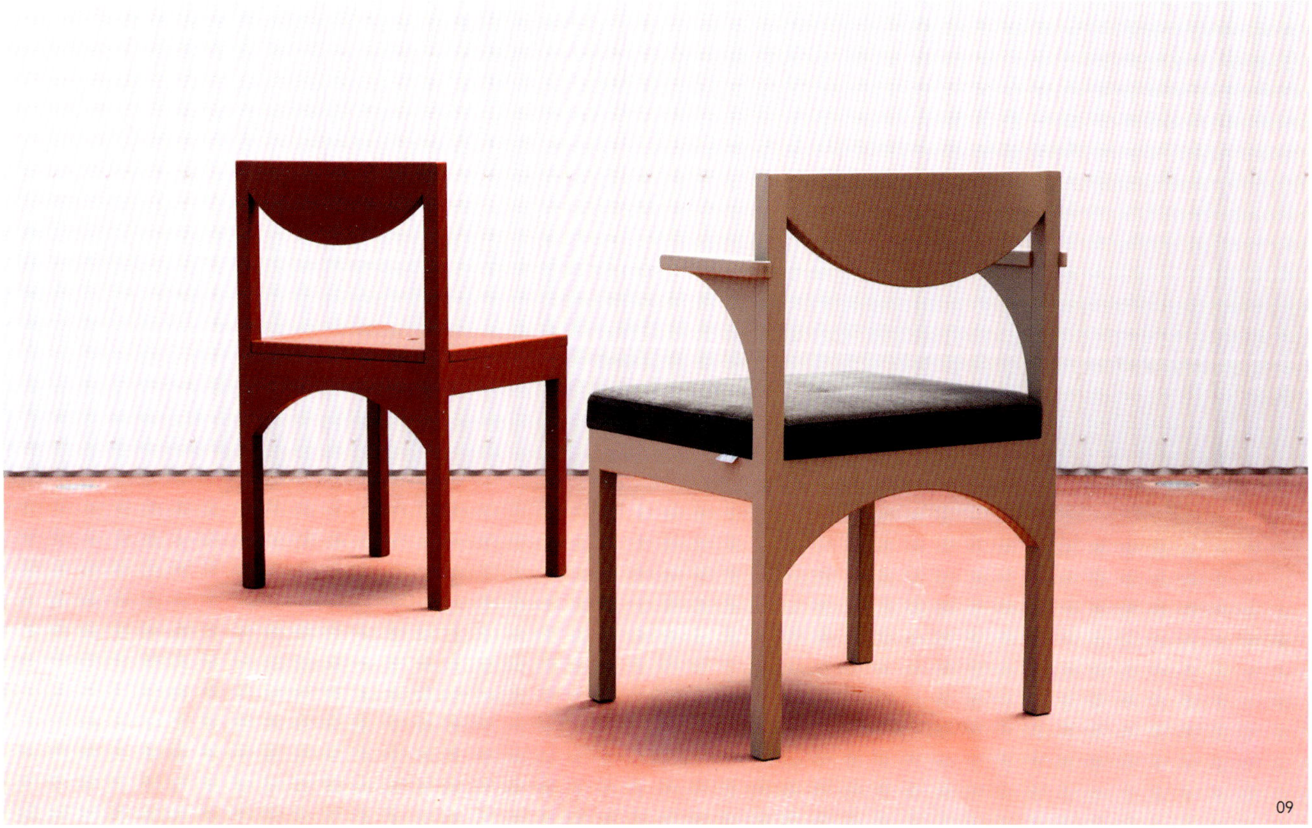

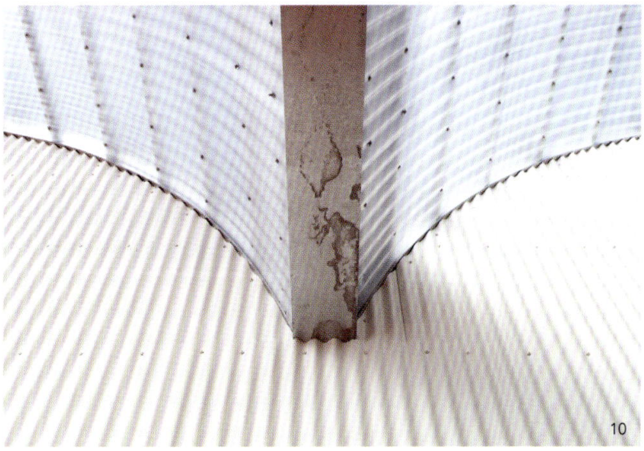

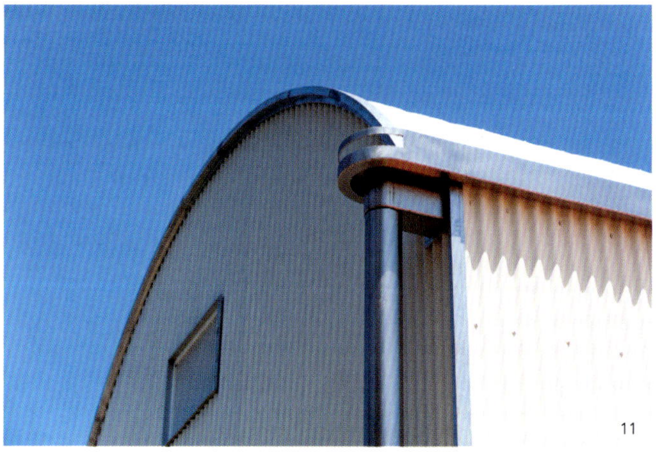

09. Chairs designed by Futatsumata
10. Junction of two arches
11. End of the rain gutter
12. Night view from the ocean
13. Ocean view from the private room

01. Facade
02-03. Interior overview

Salle de Sejour

DESIGNER Design Unit 774 / Naoya Matsumoto Design **USE** Restaurant / Dessert store **LOCATION** Osaka, Japan **AREA** 66m² **PHOTOGRAPHER** Kazuaki Michishita

This project is located on the south of Tenjoji in Osaka. It is a French cuisine "Garrett" specialty store. The old material for making crepes was quite expensive, so people stretch the buck wheat flour to resemble the crepes, and eat the wrapped variety of food.

The designer thought about representing the history of Garrett visually in the modern sense. He applies the wood, wool, cement boards, and use mortar to finish the floor, wall and ceiling. The space was directed into cleanness and simplicity.

Sketch

04. Interior view
05-08. Interior details

07

08

63

01. Facade
02. Interior overview

Cafe in the Park

DESIGNER Curiosity Inc. **USE** Restaurant / Cafe **LOCATION** Osaka, Japan **PHOTOGRAPHER** Nacasa & Partners

The space created around two large windows is a welcoming bright modern interior. The "greige" (beige plus grey) tone of interior combined natural stones and washed wood, highlighted with a metallic sculptural lighting in the ceiling. A sense of modern luxury is created with the combination of lighting and materials. The contrast between the different zones, the open space and intimate area, create the ideal setting for different customers.

In the center presented on large stones, a generation buffet is the highlight of the space, and the special lighting will emphasis the color of the food on display. The two-floor open space in the back is the ideal space for all day dining. The metal sculpture on the ceiling becomes a strong lighting feature at night, reflected on the vertical grey glass wall. Carefully designed flower arrangements are placed at different areas creating a dynamic and refined ambiance.

03. Interior details
04. Ceiling
05. Interior wall detail
06. Interior detail

① Kitchen
② Main Hall
③ Counter
④ WC

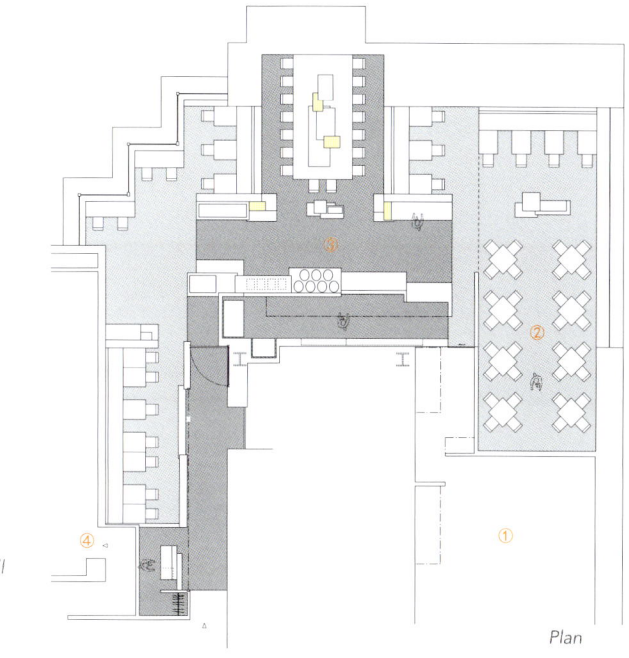

Plan

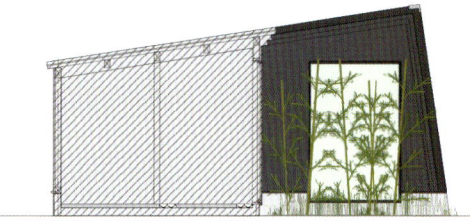

South Elevation

East Elevation

Sushi Marine

DESIGNER Tetsuya Matsumoto   **USE** Restaurant   **LOCATION** Hyogo-ken, Japan   **AREA** 67.15m²
PHOTOGRAPHER Toshiyuki Nishimatsu

This is an extension to a sushi-go-round restaurant. The old building is for sushi at reasonable prices, while the new extension is for relatively high-class dishes and wines. According to our cost and performance considerations, we decided to build the extension with wood since the new building is one-storied and smaller than the old one in scale. We avoided connecting the two buildings due to the iron frame of the old one. Instead, to connect the buildings, expansion joints were used for the approach to the extension as shown in the photos.

The extension building, which accentuates the sushi served is at the old building. In fact, sushi sales have been increased. This restaurant with two different dining spaces has entertained a diverse range of customers, including families, couples and business people for various occasions.

01. Courtyard and garden
02-04. Entrance road

05-08 Interior

① Open Courtyard
② Private Room
③ Ornate Room
④ Outside courtyard
⑤ Existing Restaurant

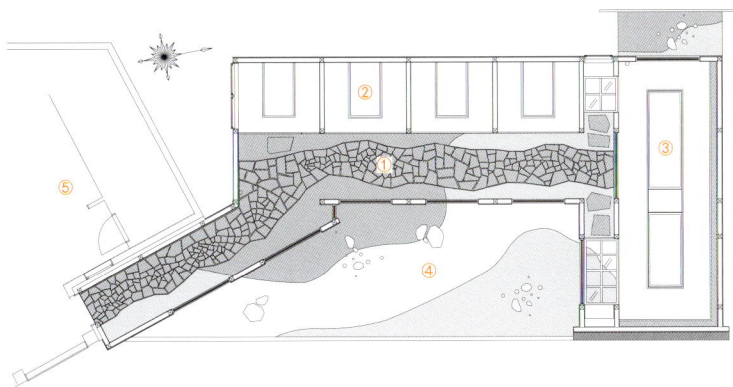

Shared Terrace

DESIGNER Hisaaki Hirawata, Tomohiro Watabe / MOMENT **USE** Bakery cafe **LOCATION** Tokyo, Japan **CLIENT** IVY, Inc. **AREA** 456m² **PHOTOGRAPHER** Nacasa & Partners

The cafe named "Shared Terrace" opens along Icho Namiki Street in Tokyo, famous for its ginkgo trees turning beautifully yellow in autumn. The concept is "Living is Sharing." That is to say, we share one, such as space, time, dish, or scene.

What embodies the concept most is the long table with 14 seats in the dining area. The customers seated at the table would happen to share communications, each dish, and a period of pleasant time. Also the sliding glass doors clear the border between the bar and deck, and make the customers and workers close. The bakery at the entrance, always fresh from the oven is on the wagons. The customers are able to enjoy hot and warm breads directly from the kitchen.

The bakery is designed moderately to keep the freshness. We hope that the rough materials, non-painted wood and steel of the wagons, stimulate the customers as if they come to the bread factory, and enjoy a direct purchase. The customers who take it out, they can enjoy having it on the stone benches in patios along the street. It is said that they can be advertisement to the passersby, who find different scenes outside from inside.

There are many areas prepared for a great numbers of customers in the "Shared Terrace". As there is no partition wall inside, it does not take a long time for the customers to get a general image of the cafe. Although the cafe space is divided into some areas, its inside looks spacious and open without any interruptions. One spacious space is to share with many. The seats placed in each divided areas; patio with stone benches, deck with outdoor seats, bakery, bar, main dining with a long table, bench seats, and low seats. In each area, the eye level is different because of the different floor level, furniture size, or chair height. The customers would spend a relaxing time as their eyes would not meet each other, and not bother each other's private time.

The usage of the intimate materials easily welcomes many customers. For instance, the vintage wooden door is set at the entrance. Non-painted natural wood is used for the wall, furniture, and floor inside. The steel wall covered with rust outside makes us think of the passage of time in nature. This makes the customers feel closer to the cafe than the usage of the new materials of the advanced technology.

01. Facade. The copper plate is being weathered into rust.
02. The stately vintage door welcomes the customers.
03. Just baked breads are placed around the entrance.
04. The cafe area with sunshine. Doors can be all open.

05. Stone bench as the minimal art of sculpture.
06. Once doors are all opened, the border between outside and inside disappears.
07. The furniture varies in height, avoiding the eyes of customers to meet each other.
08. The cozy bar counter
09. Maximum 10 customers can "share" a pleasant time at the big table in front of fireplace.

Plan

Itoman Gyomin Shokudo

DESIGNER Yamazaki Kentaro Design Workshop **USE** Restaurant **LOCATION** Itoman-shi, Okinawa, Japan **AREA** 83.78m² **PHOTOGRAPHER** Nahoko Koide, Wataru Oshiro

The Itoman Gyomin Shokudo, located in Itoman, Okinawa was conceived with the aim of supporting and promoting the local tradition and culture through its cuisine.
The restaurant is covered in Ryukyu limestone and was constructed as part of a "masonry workshop" organized by the project collaborators.
The fishermen in Itoman often constructed their own fishery grounds by hand using Ryukyu limestone. For this reason, we adopted the traditional construction method of "Nozura-Zatsuzumi" to construct the facade with the help of local workshop participants. Using the techniques of their ancestors they have imbued the structure with the pride and love of fishermen.
The restaurant seating is raised from the ground level and creates a spatial balance with the sunken gardens that surround it. The single-slab flat roof on top of the facade functions to shield the interior from the hot Okinawa sun while the wind passes freely through the interior. By choosing to make the roof from a single panel, we hope the restaurant becomes a landmark in the area and contributes to a generous landscape rooted in the culture of Itoman, Okinawa.

AWARDS
JCD DESIGN AWARD 2013, Gold Award & Makoto OIKAWA Award; GOOD DESIGN AWARD 2013; The International Architecture Award (Chicago); Japan Association of Architectural Firms Award, Chairman Prize; Design For Asia Awards 2014 (Hong Kong); Euro Shop, JAPAN SHOP Award, First Prize

01. Facade
02-03. Construction scenes
04. Interior
05. View from the exterior

06
07

① Entrance
② Table and Chairs
③ Floor Seating
④ Private Room
⑤ Kitchen
⑥ Toilet
⑦ Sunken Garden
⑧ Terrace

Plan

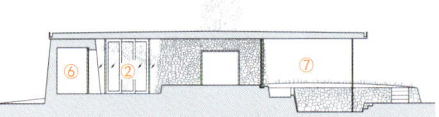 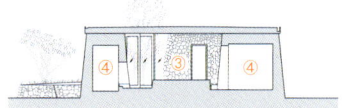

Sections

06. View from the exterior
07. Interior view
08. View from the exterior
10. Interior window view

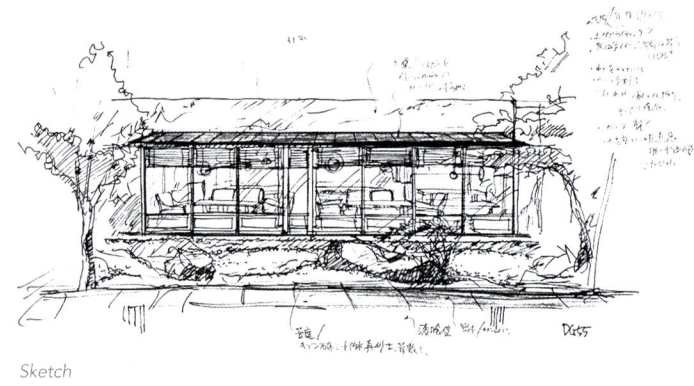

Sketch

Shubari

DESIGNER Seiji Kumamoto / designground55 **USE** Restaurant **LOCATION** Osaka, Japan **CLIENT** Shubari **AREA** 81m² **PHOTOS** Nakasa & Partners / Daisuke Shima

Authentic food serves as the crucial part of a classic restaurant. The exposure of the whole food production could be considered as a promise of great cuisine.

Japanese restaurant "Shubari" serves the traditional Japanese meal "buckwheat". The whole process of preparation and cooking is shown to the customers, from milling through paste preparation to cooking. As the whole method is traditional, through the restaurant and even at its garden, which occupies about 30% of the whole territory, traditional construction techniques are applied.

Throughout traditional and natural materials are used, such as mud wall, gypsum plastering, large size wood plank, and even the garden is using moss, as a decorating element.

The mixed design approach well presents the balance of human and nature, the interior and the landscape, the traditional and the present.

Sketch

01. Garden view from the interior
02. Facade
03-04. Interior

05-06. Interior details
07. Interior overview

07

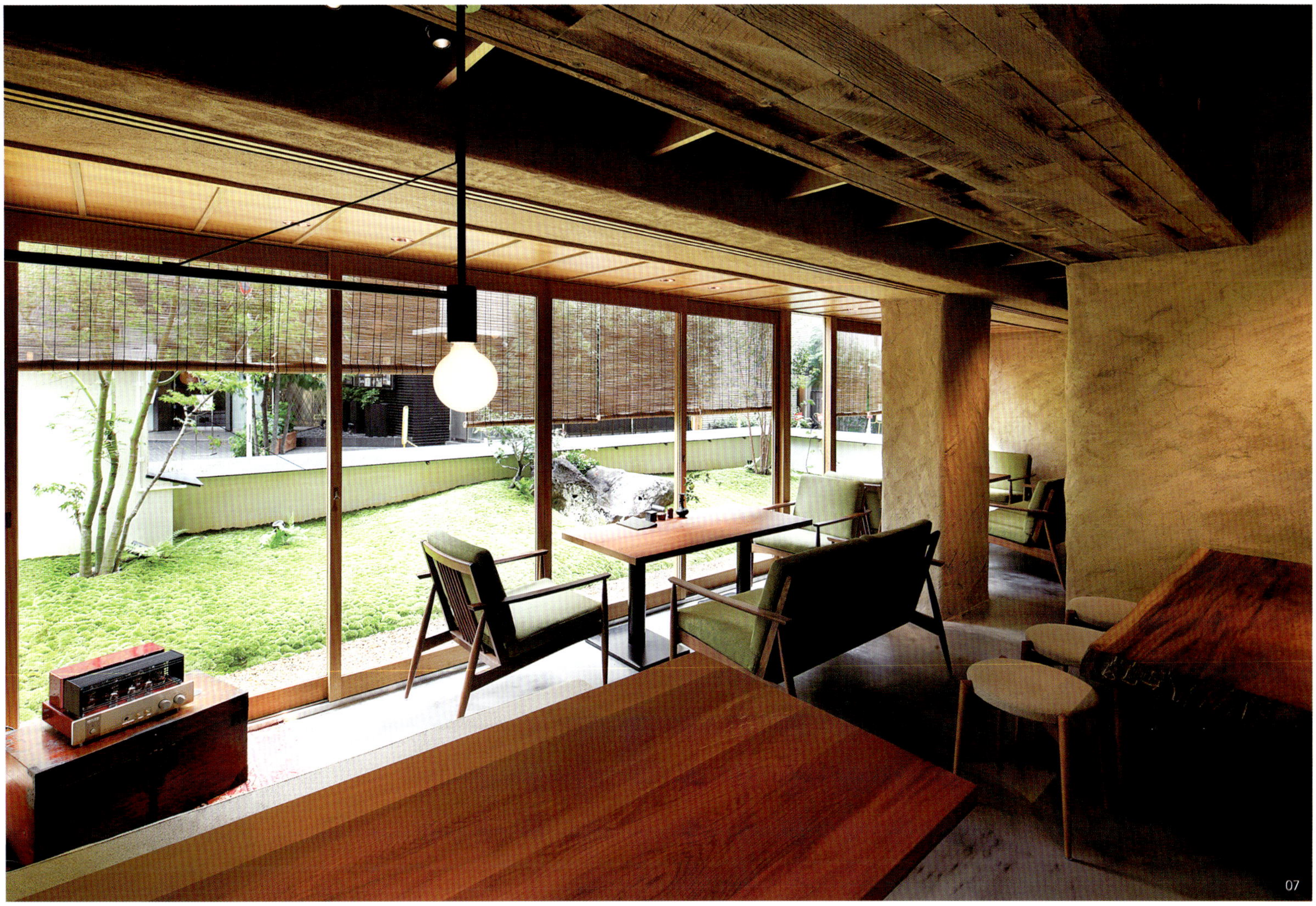

① Kitchen
② WC
③ Counter
④ Japanese Garden

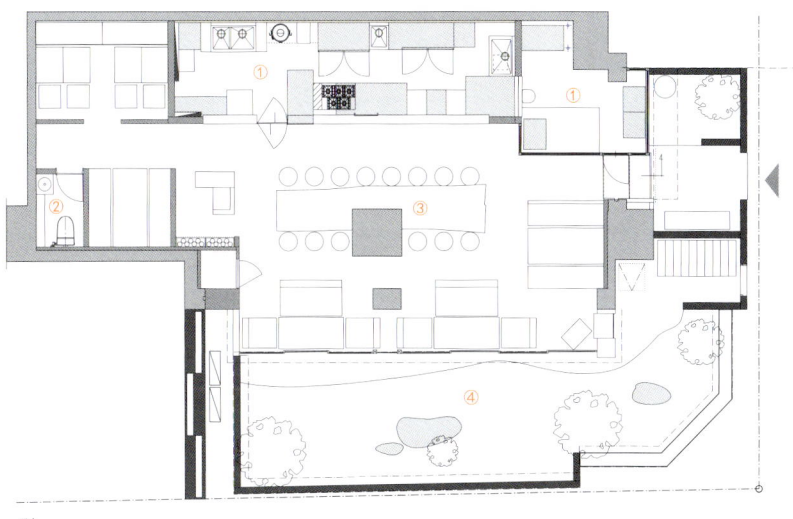

Plan

08. View from the garden
09-11. Interior details

01. Interior overview
02. Facade
03-05. Interior details

Elevation

Izakaya Tsunagi

DESIGNER Tetsuya Matsumoto **USE** Restaurant **LOCATION** Hyogo-ken, Japan **AREA** 82.6m²
PHOTOGRAPHER Toshiyuki Nishimatsu

Designers made wood materials into surface with grid pattern, and put materials together in stack layers. It eventually becomes a unique bistro facade. The exterior facade of the restaurant was installed by lighting facility. It creates a unique effect of shadow of the exterior facade.
At the point of interior design, the wall is made of marble material. The fabric curtain is not only separating each seat but also adding more interior colors and making the space more abundant. There is a great indoor Japanese-style courtyard. Tall bamboos and white gravels also make the space closer to the nature.

06-08. View from the interior
09. Entrance landscape

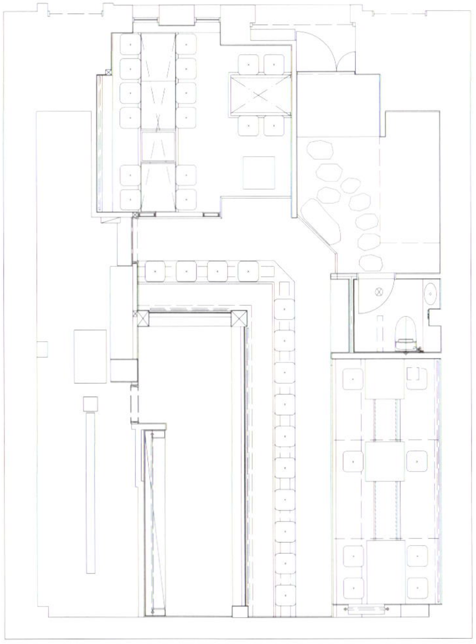

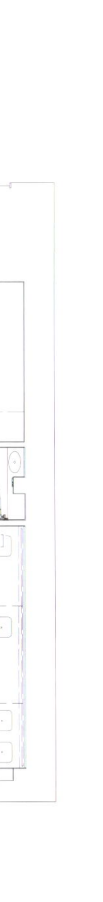

Plan

Cafe Kureon

DESIGNER Kengo Kuma & Associates **USE** Restaurant **LOCATION** Toyama city, Japan **AREA** 208,86m² **CLIENT** AKATSUKI-KUREHA LLC **PHOTOS** Kengo Kuma & Associates

Cafe Kureon is located in a park in Toyama city. The restaurant is built in an unusual wooden structure, worthy of being called wood masonry. Low-priced materials (American Pine) in standardized size of section (105mm×105mm) were piled up like stones to create a fluid, maze-looking space, as if a cave is being stretched like a network. Each part is holed with 31mmφ, and steel rod with 30mmφ vertically goes through it. Adhesives and bolts are kept at the utmost minimum so that the building can be disassembled, moved, or be added and renovated without damaging the material – a kind of "nomadic" structure, taking account of its unique location in the park.

MATERIALS
main structure wood; partly steel frame

01-02. Overview
03. Entrance
04. Interior
05. Outdoor table

06. Interior
07. Interior details
08. Overview

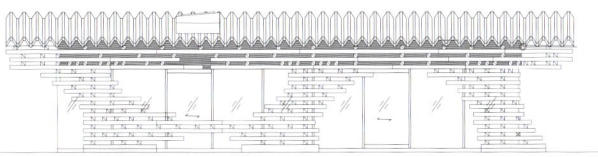
South Elevation

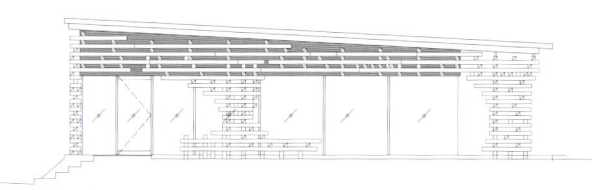
West Elevation

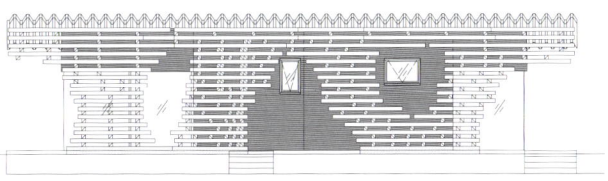
North Elevation

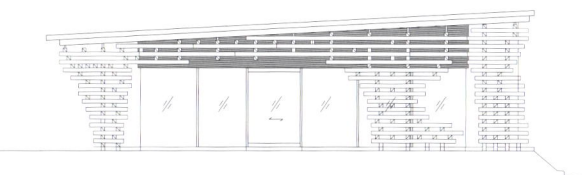
East Elevation

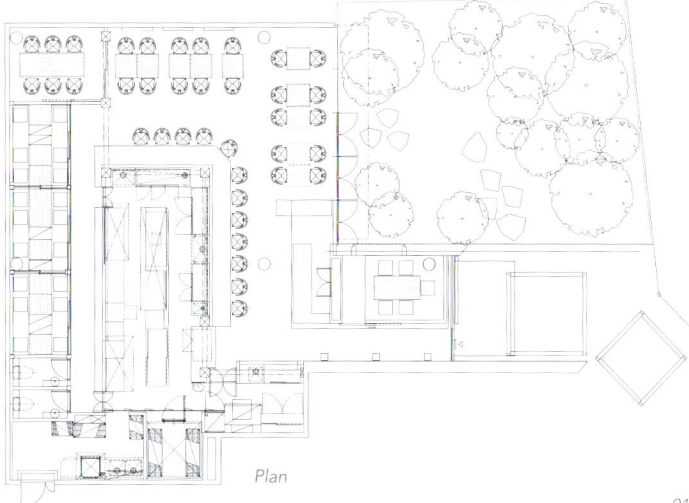

Plan

01. Approach space with a view of Japanese garden
02. The entrance with "Noren" curtain
03. Interior view
04. "Obi" decoration for ceiling structure

Fukui, Bouyourou

DESIGNER HaKo Design **USE** Restaurant **LOCATION** Minami-Aoyama, Tokyo, Japan **AREA** 163m² **PHOTOS** HaKo Design

"Fukui, Bouyourou" is a well-established Japanese-style inn facing the Sea of Japan, located at Mikuni-minato in Fukui Prefecture, and it is a new Japanese restaurant in Tokyo. Upon the start of this project, I had learnt many traditional methods of rural areas from scratch, which are high-mix low-volume production and are extraneous to mass consumption. This project incorporated these methods into its design.
In particular, I used traditional materials and techniques passed down for generations in Fukui Prefecture, such as Japanese paper craftsmen, carpenters, old house restoration specialists, lacquer artisans, and workers from antique shops, brewery and pottery. The basic concept of this project is to recreate the existing materials without using petroleum products from contemporary perspectives.

05. Interior view
06. Drink preparation space with left side. The front is the space for making "Japanese soba".
07. "Shoji" partition for Zashiki
08. The reception counter with the roof
09. Wall decorations. One is made by "Washi" artist, the other is antique uniform for the inn.
10. "Zashiki" room with hollows where people can put legs in.
11. Raised floored private room

Yoichi

DESIGNER Taiji Fujimoto / DESIGN STUDIO CROW   **USE** Restaurant   **LOCATION** Yokkaichi, Japan
AREA 235m²   **PHOTOGRAPHER** Ouchi Studio & Ryuichi Abe

"Yoichi" is located at the centre of the local shopping area in Yokkaichi city, Mie prefecture. Here is a lively place full of merchants and travelers, which used to be the major post-town of Tokaido, the most important route of Edo period. Staring from the reminiscence of prosperity as the major post-town, it is planned to become a gathering place for workers today, to revitalize the area, designed like "machiya"– traditional merchant house style where guests enjoy local sake and food in the relaxed atmosphere.

The main feature of 1st floor is the open kitchen with 9m wooden counter seating of Japanese horse chestnut. The open kitchen is visible from every seating arrangements. The open space gives vitality to the space, and create friendly atmosphere between chefs and guests. Private dining rooms on the 2nd floor can be flexible for any styles of parties and receptions.

All design elements in the space are inspired from traditional culture and local craftsmanship, such as exterior louvers inspired from traditional Japanese house, ceramic tiles and Japanese washi paper at walls, using local indigo eye and cotton "Matsuzaka Momen" for upholstery and decorative lighting fixtures.

The ceiling pattern in the private dining room is from "Ise Katagami" which is the famous local dyed paper often used as Kimono pattern. Local unglazed porcelain, attractive wall arts which are the modern interpretation of calligraphic and "ukiyo-e" woodcut prints characterize the space where guests can touch the essence of local beauties. The interior space is designed with various traditional local elements.

The designer tries to make "Yoichi" a "Home Sweet Home", a comfortable gathering place with feelings of good old days, help customers escape from modern busy live.

01. Facade
02. Counter
03. Dining Area

First Floor Plan

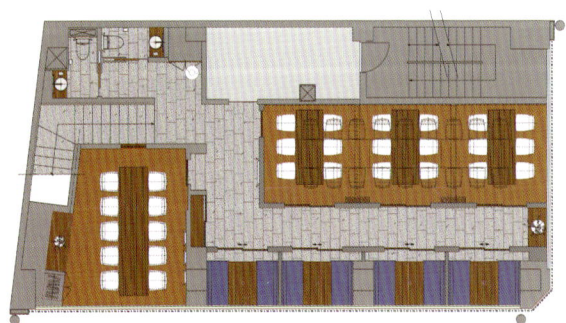
Second Floor Plan

04. Overview
05. Corridor
06. Private Dining Room 1
07. Private Dining Room 2

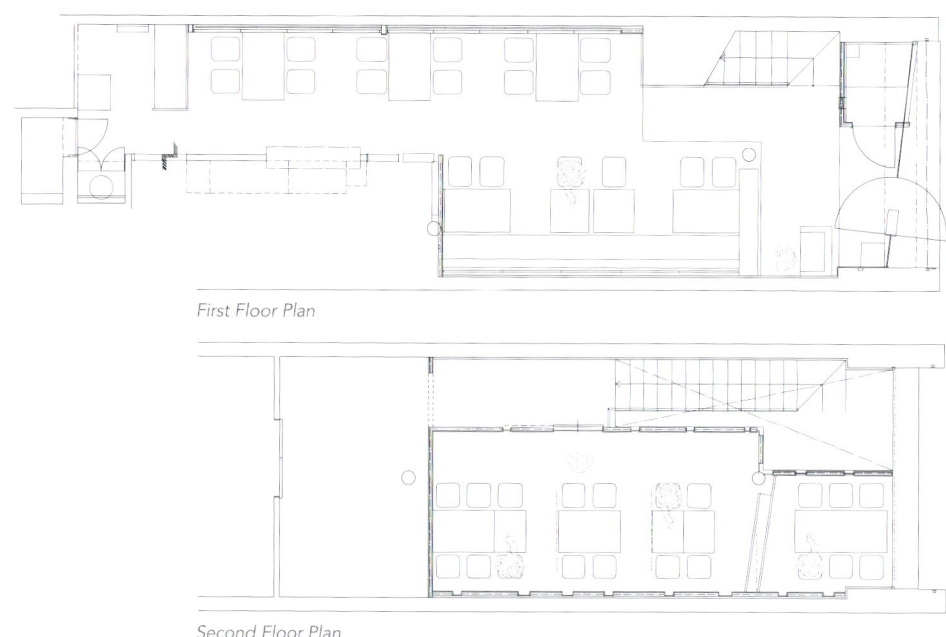

First Floor Plan

Second Floor Plan

Hana-Soba Yu

DESIGNER Tetsuya Matsumoto / Matsuya Art-Works **USE** Restaurant **LOCATION** Himeji, Japan
AREA 105.1m² **PHOTOS** Toshiyuki Nishimatsu

This is the renovation of a wooden building, constructed about 70 years ago. The owner is a maker of homemade buckwheat noodles. He is also a potter. His wish was to have a space built in his store to display his works.

At the entrance, the designer placed the furniture for displaying his works. One could see the interior of the store beyond that display. The designer tiled the wall behind the sofa with the tiles that pay homage to the exquisite shade of green uniquely achieved by the traditional ceramic technique called "Igayaki".

01-02. Interior overview
03. Ceramic display

04-07. Interior details

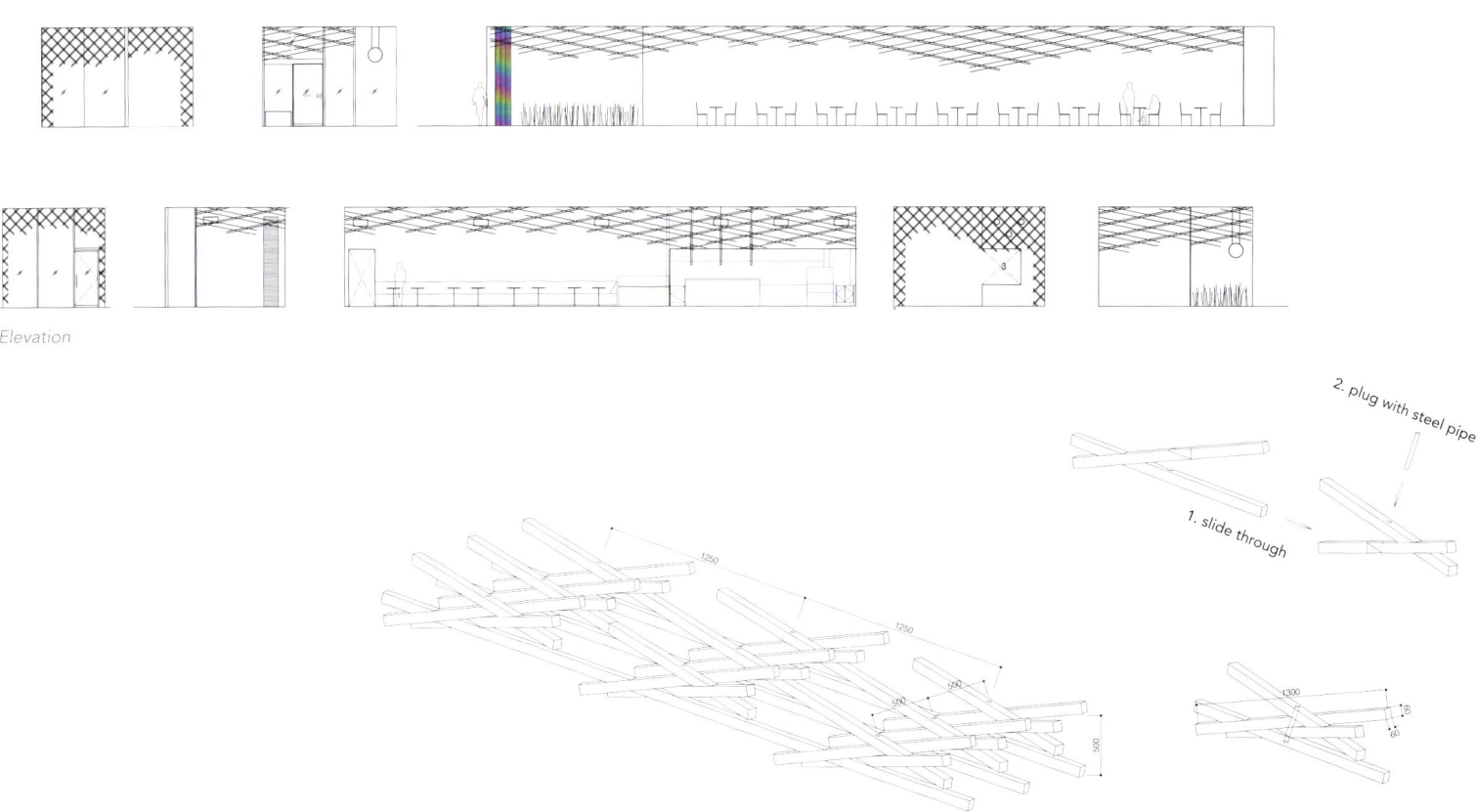

Elevation

Starbucks Coffee at Dazaifu Tenmangu

DESIGNER Kengo Kuma & Associates **USE** Cafe **LOCATION** Omotesando, Tokyo, Japan **CLIENT** Manten Corporation **AREA** 210.03m² **PHOTOS** Kengo Kuma & Associates

The location of Starbucks Coffee is somehow characteristic, as it stands on the main approach to the Dazaifu Tenmangu, one of the most major shrines in Japan. Established in 919 A.D., the shrine has been worshiped as "the God for Examination," and receives about 2 million visitors a year who wish their success. Along the main path to the shrine, there are traditional Japanese buildings in one or two storeys. The project aimed to make a structure that harmonizes with such a townscape, using a unique system of weaving thin woods diagonally.

The building is made of 2,000 stick-like parts between 3m to 4m length and a 6cm section. Total length of the sticks reached are as far as 4.4km. We had experimented with the weaving of sticks for the project of Chidori and GC Prostho Museum Research Center, and this time we tried the diagonal weaving in order to bring in a sense of direction and fluidity. Three sticks are joined at one point in Chidori and GC, while in Starbucks four steps come to one point because of the diagonal – a more complicated joint. We solved the problem by slightly changing positions of the fulcrums, and dividing the four sticks into two groups to avoid concentration on a single point. Piling up of small parts from the ground was highly developed in the traditional architecture of Japan and China. This time the method was greatly improved in combination with state-of-the the-art technology so that people are brought further into the architecture. It is a fluid, cave-like space.

01

01. Facade
02-03. Interior details

04. View from the interior
05-06. Interior details

05
06

① Entrance
② Cafe Seating
③ Back Bar
④ Work Room
⑤ Managers' Room
⑥ WC
⑦ Machine Room
⑧ Garden
⑨ Air Conditioning Unit

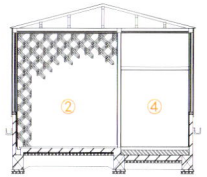

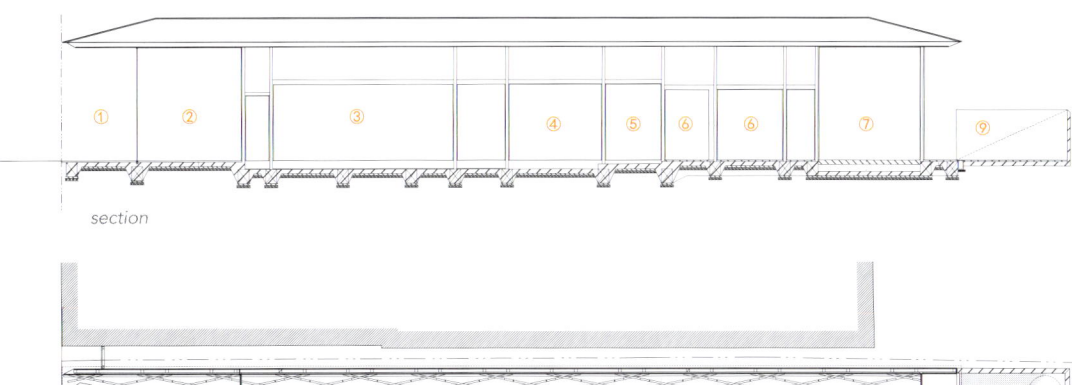

section

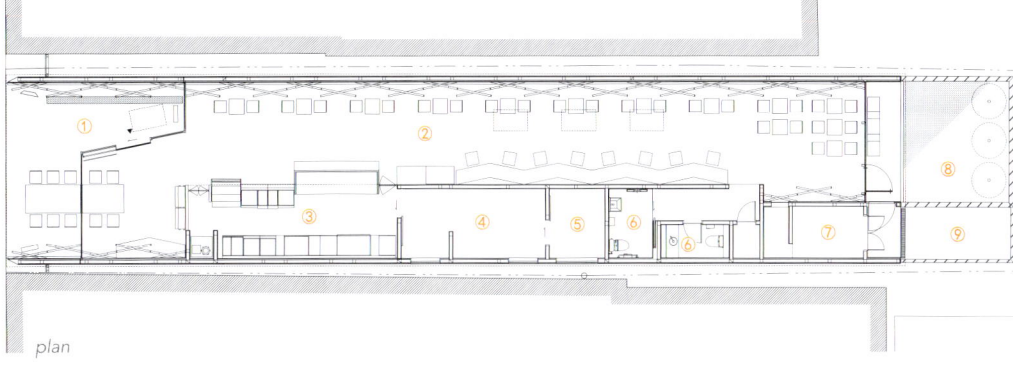

plan

Tsuruichi Yakiniku

DESIGNER Golucci International Design **USE** Restaurant **LOCATION** Beijing, China **CLIENT** Tsuruichi Yakiniku **PHOTOGRAPHER** Sun Xiangyu

Tsuruichi Yakiniku is a very popular Japanese Yakinikum restaurant famous for its wonderful beef barbecue. It is located in Tsuruichi area, the east of Osaka, where many Korean families live among the local Japanese households, therefore the unique and diverse culture is found there. Tsuruichi, in Japanese, means "the top one in Tsuruichi area", and actually it is the first Yakinikum restaurant in this area in the recent hundred years.

We used strip-type partition board in this project, because it is always used in Japanese architecture. In fact, the use of numerous close-grained stripes, to some extent, satisfied the aesthetics of the Japanese people, because we found an interesting way of drawing rains in Ukiyo-e (a famous Japanese painting collection) when we were finding materials and inspiration for the design: the artist Utagawa Hiroshige used dense strips to paint the pouring rains in Summer in the picture named Sudden Rain Falling on the Bridge of his Hundred Beautiful Sceneries in Edo Era collection. The sudden change of weather and the instant reactions of pedestrians were captured by the artist and showed in the pictures, making a great painting collection and even attracting Vincent van Gogh's attention; therefore the picture collection became well-known in the world. This way of painting rain is unique also because you can neither see it in the Western paintings nor in Chinese ink paintings.

In the design, the restaurant echoes the crowded streets and dense buildings: the two entrances are at the gable walls, and when you are inside the restaurant, the triangle slope crest immediately comes to your sight. Also, we intentionally lower the eaves in order to use the triangle roof to indicate the relationship between Japanese architecture and the hill of woods. In Japanese architecture circle, if the entrance is in the gable wall, it is called "tsuma iri"; if the entrance is under the eave, it's called "hira iri". The eave of this restaurant is only 2.1m, which is very low even for a residential building, let alone a restaurant, a public building. So we were claimed by the developer that we have no common sense of architecture, and the customers are able to touch the roof as long as they stretch their arms. But we explained to them that we made the eave so low is because we want to make the walls hidded by the eaves and their shades. In this way, the triangle roof can stand out and makes the restaurant look like a small hill among the modern buildings in the city.

01-02. Entrance
03. View from the exterior

① Landscape
② Open Dining Area
③ Private Dining Room
④ Bar
⑤ Kitchen

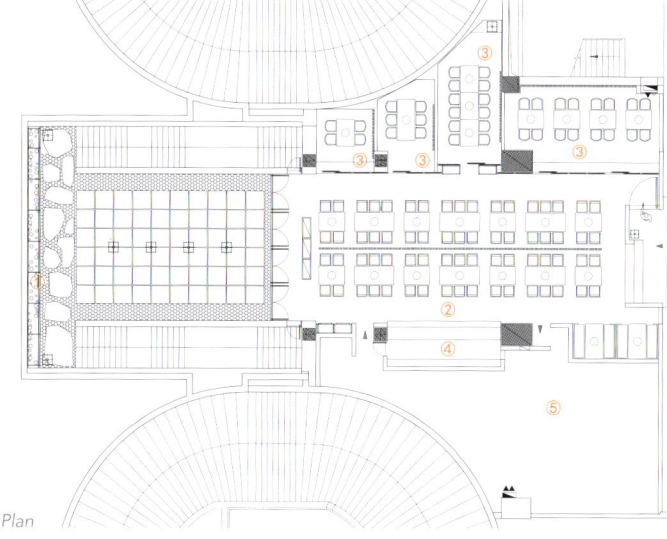

Plan

04. The ceiling feature
05-06. Interior details

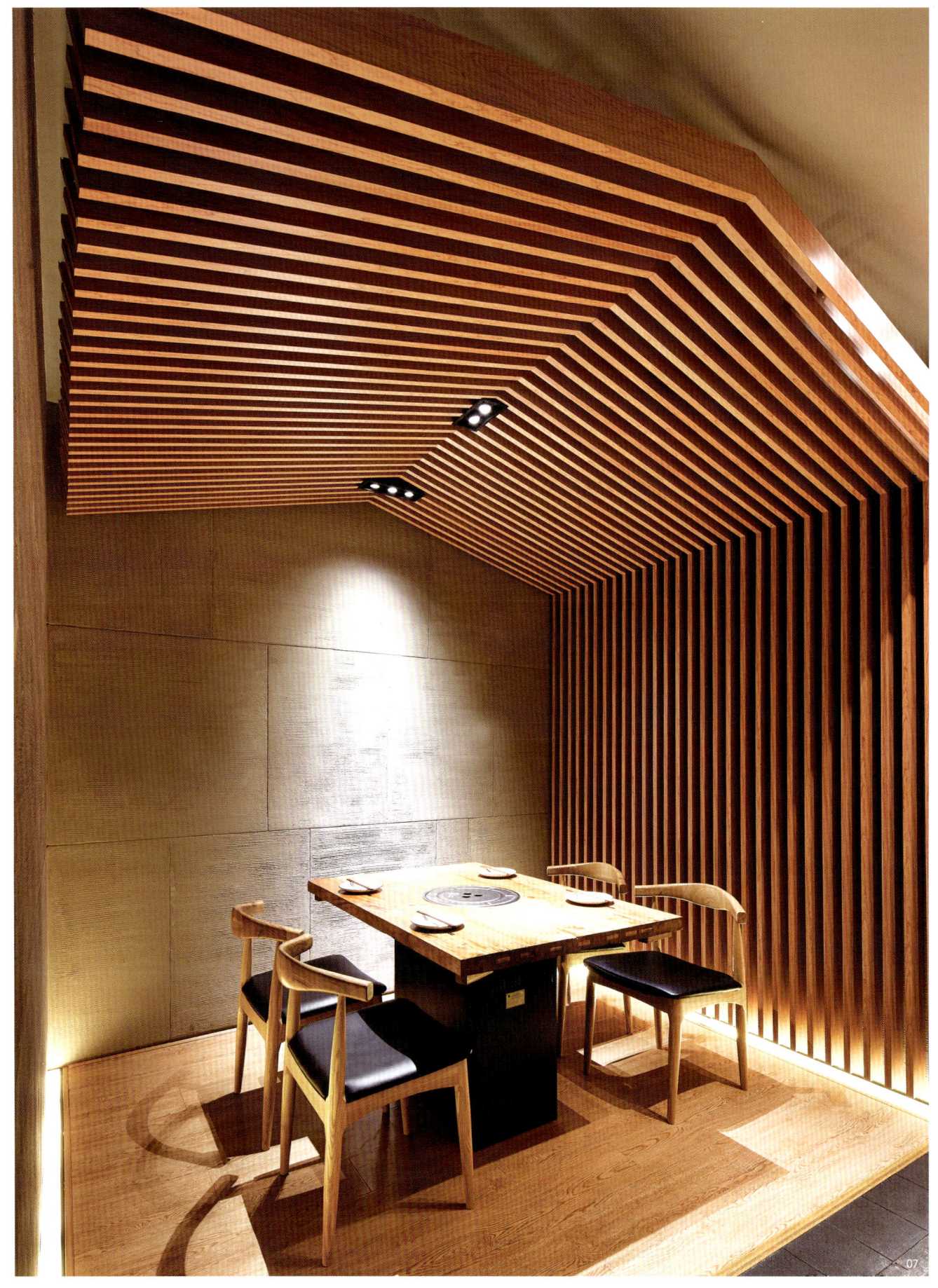

07-09. Dining area details

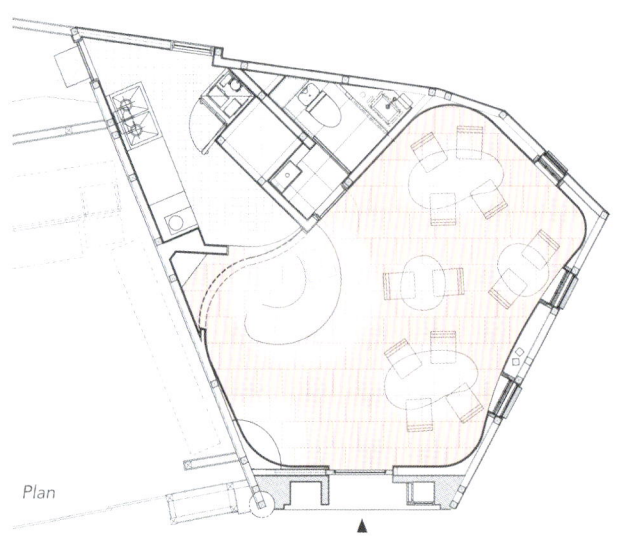
Plan

Cha no Chimoto

DESIGNER Hiroyuki Ogawa, Erika Okamoto / Hiroyuki Ogawa Architects Inc. **USE** Cafe / Shop
LOCATION Kanagawa, Japan **AREA** 34.43m² **PHOTOGRAPHER** T. Hiraga

This project is a Japanese confectionery and tea shop. The site in Hakone is well-known from long ago as a hot spring district. In Hakone, there is a white western-style building that was constructed in the early 20th century, and this building has become a local landmark.

Our client, the Japanese confectioner "Chimoto", has a history stretching back more than 60 years, and they are currently operating this building. The name "Chimoto" comes from "a thousand cherry blossoms". It is said that the founder named it after getting the idea from the title of "Yoshitune Senbon zakura", a play in the traditional Japanese performing art of Kabuki.

Chimoto's main attraction is a soft, white rice cake called "Yumochi", and customers visit the shop from all over Japan in search of it. We worked on the preservative repairs of this locally important building, as well as the interior of our client's new Japanese confectionery and tea house "Cha no Chimoto". Our design goal was to use the cherry blossom symbol of Chimoto to evoke a traditional Japanese spirit and create new expressions without falling into nostalgia for the old days.

We utilized the following specific methods to achieve our goal.

First of all, for walls, we covered the surfaces that had become warped by repeated extensions and alterations to the building with curved walls and finished them with diatomite plaster. By doing so, we changed the disharmonious surfaces to give an impression of softness.

Second, for the windows, we installed glass windows with sliding paper screens called "yukimi shouji", and put representations of cherry trees on the paper screens. These paper screens symbolically link the scenery visible through the window with the interior.

Additionally, for the guest seating tables and large bowl-shaped counter, we replaced the traditional Japanese technique of lacquering with a modern polyester resin material. Gauze cut into the shape of cherry blossom petals was arranged on the surface of the furniture and coated with polyester resin, followed by a process of repeated polishing to give the cherry blossom petals a sense of depth.

As a result, we succeeded in suggesting a spring scene of fluttering cherry petals with the cherry blossom motif used throughout and suggesting the "Yumochi" made by Chimoto with the soft white walls and curves of the furniture.

01. Entrance
02. Facade
03. Interior

PRODUCTION PROCESS OF "CHERRY BLOSSOMS PATTERN TABLE"

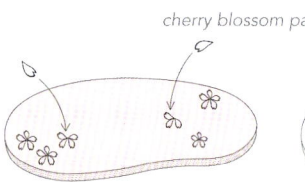
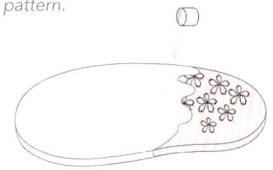
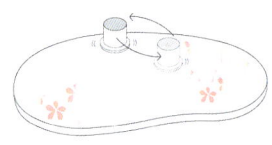

1. Fix the place of the cherry blossom pattern.
Give a coat of primer to a wooden table, place the gauze where you have previously cut the pattern for the petals of the cherry blossoms on top of it, and apply transparent polyester resin on top of it to fix it in place.

2. Apply resin.
Apply polyester resin mixed with white paint.

3. Express depth by polishing.
Polishing the surface will thin the white resin so the original color underneath becomes faintly visible. In order to create the illusion of depth, as if it was enveloped in mist, repeat the process of applying white resin and then polishing 2 or 3 times, and finish with a coat of urethane.

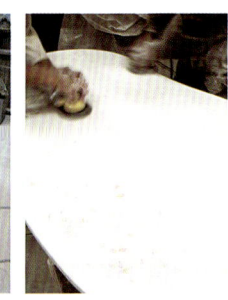

04. Interior
05-06. Table details
07. Floor detail
08. Interior

Ikibana Restaurant

DESIGNER Oliver Franz Schmidt, Natali Canas del Pozo / EL EQUIPO CREATIVO   **USE** Restaurant
LOCATION Barcelona, Spain   **AREA** 278m²   **PHOTOGRAPHER** Adrià Goula

The Ikibana restaurant offers a fusion of Japanese and Brazilian gastronomies, two cultures that seem so antagonistic: quiet and minimalist the first, exuberant and bustling the second. One of the biggest conceptual challenges during the design of the restaurant was to find shared singularities between these two cultures. Being a great challenge, it also became the leitmotif of the project, as we discovered that the landscape was an extremely important element in both cultures, and we decided to extol this element in the design of the space and create an artificial landscape.

On the one hand Brazil represents an extraordinary lush landscape, while Brazilian life style absorbs and reflects this voluptuousness, always cheerful and full of color. On the other, traditional Japanese paintings, as well as the visual and dramatic arts, are full of references to their landscape. The art of flower arrangement known as Ikebana is one of the examples of this respect for nature deeply rooted in Japanese culture, and gives its name to the restaurant and inspiration to its design.

Our client is looking for a restaurant where people would not only taste the food and look at the space, but could also feel it, listen to and smell it. They wanted to escape from the minimal Japanese space, and approach a more organic and feminine atmosphere, cozy, glamorous and spectacular at the same time.

The result is a sinuous landscape created by different program elements or islands. On the one hand, bars and kitchens are divided and distributed around the restaurant, creating intensity nodes spread throughout the space. On the other hand, guests are sitting in the interior of colorful bowls. These islands are embraced by a fluid space which meanders around the restaurant, producing infinite angles of vision and allowing the constant movement of the waiters presenting the food to liven the atmosphere.

These Ikebana artistic arrangements look for the right proportion, composition and equilibrium among three elements: wood, leaves and flowers. The results are light, elegant and static compositions that simulate movement, premises in which our design will be articulated.

The wooden element in our design comes with the spectacular ceiling designed as a forest of entwined branches, becoming one of the main protagonists of the space. The light crosses the ceiling projecting a warm tinkling of lights and shadows on every surface of the restaurant.

As a counterpoint to the wood, the vegetal or green element can be found inside the display windows, acting as a curtain that diffuses the light and the vision between the interior and the street.

In a lower proportion, but not less important, the necessary color element in the Ikebana arrangements comes with the tables. Their design brings an explosion of fresh and tropical colors: lemon yellow, lime green, passion red. Its organic shape reminds us of a petal and can be easily adapted for groups, producing a new color composition with each new table arrangement.

01. View from the street
02. Sushi bar

The following are the different elements we apply in the project:

THE CEILING: The roof was made out of a tropical wood called "Mongoy". The roof was only designed with 8 different "elements" or "sheets", which was placed in different positions and directions that compose the complexity of the whole. A 3D digital model was first created in our studio, and from this model 8 different metal casts or moulds were built in the workshop, which helped shape the final laminated wooden sheets.

THE PETAL TABLES: We were looking for a ceramic-like finish for the tables, a natural handmade feeling that would make each table a slightly different piece. Finally the MDF wooden pieces were painted manually with a specific paint, reproducing an antique craftsman technique of ceramic painting, were different layers of paint were put on top of each other in order to get a transparency between colors, small delicate fissures and cracks, and a different result in each table. The final finishing of the tables is bright and shiny as a counterpoint to the general natural and mate finishing of the restaurant. During the day they reflect the natural light of the exterior and the moving shadows of the vegetal facade; during the night their color explodes.

THE WINDOW PANELS: Different layers of glass were laminated, but in the process of lamination we tried to produce imperfections or "bubbles" between the layers. These bubbles give the glass a translucent and watery feeling and make each panel slightly different as well.

VEGETAL INSTALATIONS OR IKEBANAS: On top of the sushi bar we find a flower installation composed by natural dry branches of trees and artificial white flowers, which we ended up calling "the cloud". We designed this element in collaboration with "Bossvi", which is a flower-shop in Barcelona. We also designed an specific lighting system for "the cloud" in collaboration with "La Invisible", a lighting designer in Barcelona. The intensity of the lighting system varies in time, producing a movement in the installation, an organic life feeling; something similar to what happens when real clouds pass in front of the sun produces subtle variations of natural light. The "patio" or indoor garden behind the sushi bar was also an installation designed in collaboration with "Bossvi", together with the facade installations. All of them where composed by a combination of natural dry branches, roots and leaves, together with a few fantasy flowers.

THE GASTRONOMY: In 1908 "Kasato Maru", a passenger boat, reached Brazil with the first Japanese immigrants. With them came the esteemed ingredients and recipes of a far-off, exotic land which until that time had been unknown. Over a hundred years later, the Japanese-Brazilian culinary tradition is famous worldwide and has its own strong identity. Two cultures which have been able to combine tastes, ingredients and textures, create a very special gastronomy.

03. View from the entrance
04. Bathroom
05. Ikebana's floral arrangement
06. Detail from the ceiling and the benches

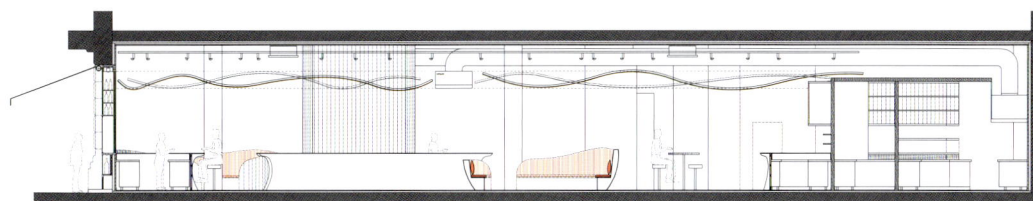

Section

07. Petal table design
08. Facade floral arrangement
09. General view
10. Sitting bowls
11. General view

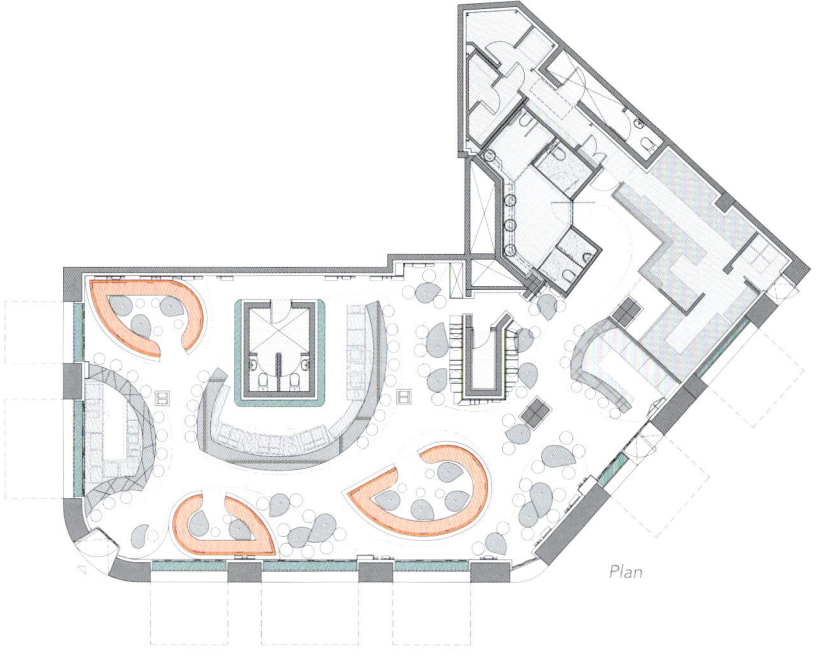

Plan

Kaiseki Yoshiyuki & Horse's Mouth

DESIGNER Asylum   **USE** Restaurant / Bar   **LOCATION** Singapore   **PHOTOS** Asylum

Within a single space, a restaurant and a bar are designed intelligently adjacent to each other. Despite both being of Japanese influences, each of them carries distinct identities, Kaiseki Yoshiyuki has a touch of elegance, while Horse's Mouth eludes a sense of fun.

Kaiseki Yoshiyuki is a Japanese restaurant located in the upscale district of Orchard Road in Singapore. A culinary art form of the highest degree, kaiseki-ryori first originated from 16th century tea ceremony rituals. Kaiseki Yoshiyuki recreates the kaiseki-ryori dining experience in Singapore by serving intricate multi-course creations made from fresh seasonal ingredients in a classic yet modern setting.

The spatial design approach of Kaiseki Yoshiyuki alludes to the restaurant's practice of reinterpreting kaiseki-ryori's traditional methods using contemporary avenues. At the entrance, leading the way into Kaiseki Yoshiyuki, roof tiles are unexpectedly clad against the walls, paying homage to the temples of Kyoto, where kaiseki-ryori was first served. Within the counter dining area, ash panelled geometrical forms cast intriguing details on the walls of the warmly lit interior. Classic yet contemporary counter style dining rooms set the stage for guests to fully savor the sensorial experience — where taste, texture and presentation seamlessly unite.

Located within the premises is Horse's Mouth, a bar inspired by the underground personality of the Japanese izakaya. Exiting Kaiseki Yoshiyuki to the bar, the immediate vision of 3000 hand-folded origami sakura flowers across three glass displays create an explosion of vibrant colors amidst the dark leather seats and deep wooden tables. Adjacent to the origami flower displays, a grid of shelves house a textural mix of used wood, akin to a well-stocked library of books.

01. Dining Area
02. Entering Kaiseki Yoshiyuki
03. Library Installation Made of Used Wood Blocks
04. Roof Tile Inspired Walls

05. The Horse's Mouth Lounge
06. Origami Installation
07. The Horse's Mouth Bar

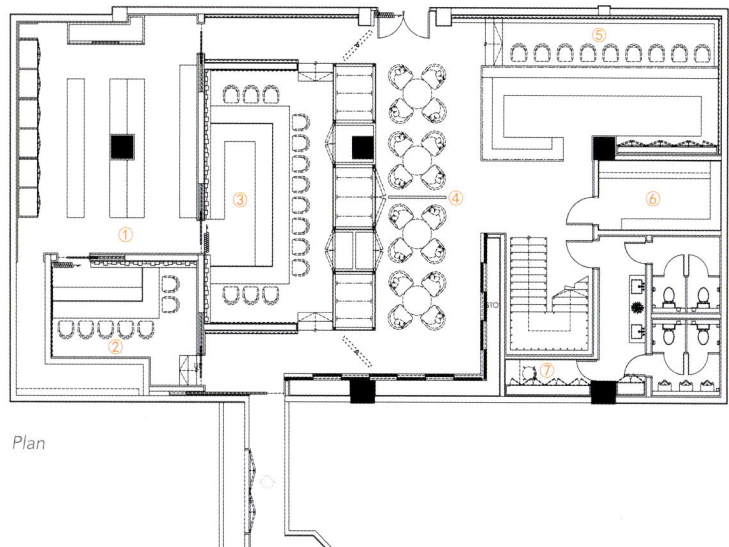

Plan

① Kitchen
② Private Room
③ Kaiseki Yoshiyuki Dining Counter
④ Lounge Dining
⑤ Bar Lounge
⑥ Storage For Beverages
⑦ Office

01. Interior overview
02. Staircase
03. Interior details

HAMA

DESIGNER k-studio **USE** Restaurant **LOCATION** Athens, Greece **AREA** 200m²
PHOTOGRAPHER Yiorgos Kordakis

HAMA is a Japanese-Brazilian restaurant, located in the southern suburbs of Athens. The concept was influenced by the philosophy of the traditional Japanese house layout, reaching a balance between open space and closed internal space. The design of the layout of Hama focuses open, social space near the entrance and bar, whilst natural bamboo screens enclose several small areas giving them privacy. To achieve a gradient between open, social and intimate, private space we raised several individual dining rooms up above the ground floor, where, like glowing bamboo lanterns they overlook the main space below, connected by suspended steel walkways. As if sitting high within a bamboo forest, diners are subtly screened from view yet remain connected to the ambience. These "lanterns" are stacked on top of each other providing partially enclosed corners of space whilst maintaining the connection to the open dining area.
The lighting is directed and focused, bringing out the beauty of the bamboo and accentuating the contrast between its warmth and the dark steel and floor.

MATERIALS
epoxy flooring, black steel panels, bamboo canes and flooring, brass

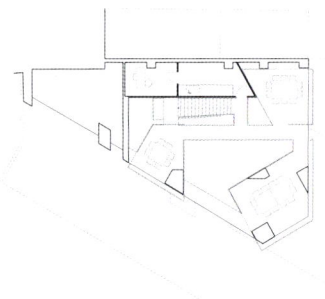
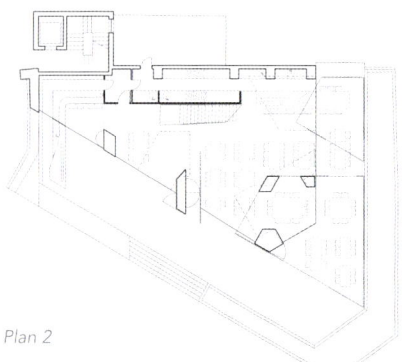
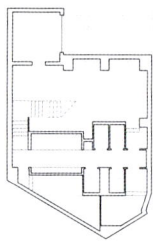

Plan 1　　　　　　　　　　Plan 2　　　　　　　　　　Plan 3

04-06. Interior details

07-10. Iconic bamboo materials and structures

① Entry
② Dining Area
③ Drinks
④ Storage
⑤ Back of House
⑥ Bar

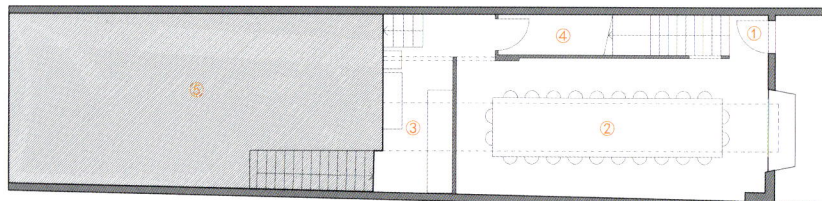

First Floor Plan

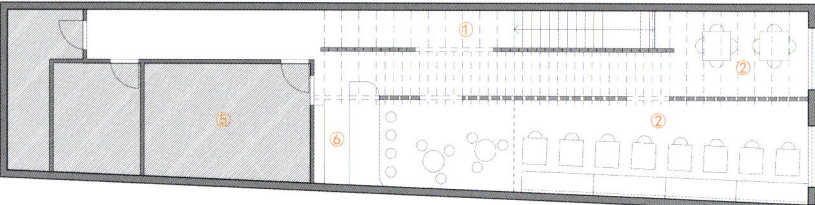

Second Floor Plan

Uchi Lounge

DESIGNER Facet Studio   **USE** Restaurant   **LOCATION** Sydney, Australia   **AREA** 155m²
PHOTOGRAPHER Andrew Chung

For nostalgic atmosphere and modern design, TIME is the only commonality between these two opposing concepts. Under its majestic flow, we opted to design ways to perceive this "time-flow" with 2 floors of Uchi Lounge – as though there are two speeds of time-flow within the same restaurant.

Uchi Lounge 01

13m long ribbon of light floating in the space with no structural support in its length. Massive 8.4mx1.6m concrete tables are firmly established at the center of the space. By structuring the space with measures unimaginable in normal restaurants, people are overwhelmed by unusual scale, hence paralyzed about scale reference. The walls and ceiling painted in boundless black seem to continue into eternity, as though the ceiling does not exist, only the weightless plane of light hovering above. "Space" becomes an abstract concept as common references fail. At this point of time, the cuisine on the table, in front of the eyes, is the only reality; the moment of "eating" is where all senses concentrate.

Uchi Lounge 02

An existing Japanese restaurant popular with regular customers captured the regulars with, not only delicious cuisine, but also the indefinably nostalgia-filled space.
To enhance the appreciation of cuisine, we designed a new circulation path from entry to table, by "repeating" 100-year-old recycled bricks and rustic raw steel - a tunnel to enhance expectation towards the cuisines when proceeding towards the table. Longer the distance, more room for enhancing this expectation.
The brick screen continued for a lengthy 15m, punctured with alternating 1/3 and 1/4 of the wall length. Steel louvers correspond with rhythm of punctures by spacing at 1 or 2 bricks, resulting in repetitive rhythm of light and shadow in the tunnel. This repetitive rhythm enhances expectation, and sensitivity to taste. When arriving at the table, it is when desire for cuisine peaks.

01. Looking at the central table from the front. The space sandwiched between a 13m-long, ribbon-shaped light and solid, concrete table becomes the "conceptual space" within the surrounding darkness, which enables patrons to concentrate on tasting the cuisine.
02. Looking from the back of the restaurant towards its front window, as if the light is projecting to the outside.
03. Close up of the brick screen. Texture of the 100-year-old recycled bricks; the solid / void composition and shadow effect animate the space and provide a rich back drop to the cuisine.
04. Looking at the entry staircase from the counter. Zoning in the restaurant is apparent; entry-circulation-dining from left to right.

05. Looking at the group dining area from the main dining area, with the circulation "tunnel" in between. The raw steel louvers extend over the group dining area, providing a different intimacy for the space.
06. Looking from the group dining area towards the circulations "tunnel". Raw steel louvers over continuing from the "tunnel" cater for a more intimate atmosphere.
07. Looking at top of the entry staircase from the bar / drinks area. Brick screen made of 100-year-old recycled bricks provides visual connection between spaces whilst maintaining clarity of zoning in the restaurant.
08. Main circulation spine in the restaurant. It is framed by brick walls of different characters on both sides, with raw steel louvers overhead. Together with light/shadow effect, this "tunnel" amplifies patrons' anticipation towards the cuisine.
09. Looking at the group dining area from the circulation "tunnel". Raw steel louvers over continuing from the "tunnel" cater for a more intimate atmosphere.

① Kitchen
② Bathrooms
③ Bar
④ Hallway
⑤ Entrance

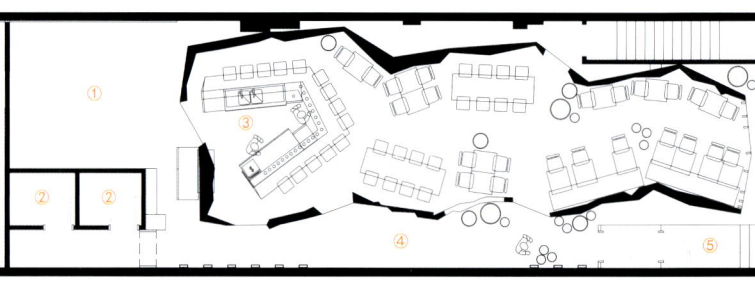

Plan

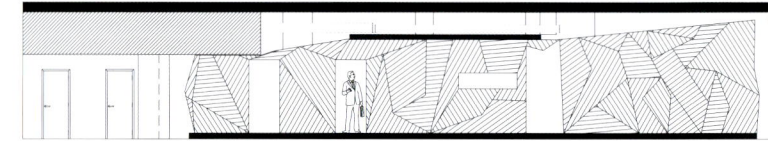

Elevation

Entrance Wall and Ceiling

Izakaya Kinoya

DESIGNER Jean de Lessard **USE** Restaurant **LOCATION** Montreal, Canada **CLIENT** Kinoya
AREA 139.35m² **PHOTOGRAPHER** Adrien Williams

For its latest Kinoya, interior designer Jean de Lessard has tapped into the sources to emulate in his design the primary spirit, function and aesthetics of the izakaya, as the latter was originally an informal place where people drank beer and enjoyed sake. The transformation is particularly unusual that it explores through extreme design intimacy in relationships between people, making of Kinoya a true representation of the unique approach the designer has developed about the different ways of occupying a space.

The notion of confinement is staged with simplicity using fractal geometry and the broken line: a box whose shape recalls an articulated snake now fills the inside of the black box where the previous Kinoya only remain the floral patterns. The box creates a break between the known / predictable (the outside world, the opening) and the unknown / unpredictable (chaotic enclosed interior, full of nooks and crannies). "For a space to become Event or Emotion, it must generate its own energy. I designed an enclosed space that is totally focused on the business of partying. The design elements are deliberately oppressive or aggressive, so that it is anarchic, rough and where we are loudly heckled", explains Jean de Lessard. The vertical drop of 4 to 5 feet between the front and rear parts of the ceiling contributes to the cocoon effect.

The place is always full since the opening, despite the fact that one must stand shoulder to shoulder. The soft lighting and the cozy atmosphere makes it a friendly environment where the smell of wood mingles pleasantly with the aromas of mouth-watering dishes.

The space, such as how one could figure what the interior of origami looks like, is composed of triangles of various sizes, crookedly placed in a random fashion. "Jean told me what he wanted to feel in this place where one had to be cramped also. It's a fantasy cave where people are in a constant visual

01. Exterior view of the wood box
02. Inside of the restaurant
03. Wood shelves
04. Flags and Lights details

exploration mode", says artist carpenter Dominic Samson, Solution durable, who built the structure, a piece of work he's proud of and that he describes as uplifting.

A durable material, wood has an exceptional capacity of resonance and absorption. The irregularity and angularity of the surfaces further deflect sound waves, helping to muffle the ambient noise. The reused wood from barns is local and covers an area that represents 4,500 square feet. Boards of hemlock and white spruce of different width and thickness were installed in all directions. If this strengthens the idea of chaos, on the other end the glued-laminated technique used for the installation provides in turn a perfect finish.

The uncouth-tavern style decoration is left to its simplest expression: the furniture and lighting were salvaged from previous Kinoya, drawings and graffiti offend the eye and confirm the urban character of the establishment. Kakemono

banners that are used to hide the street also perpetuate the Japanese tradition.
In Japan, an izakaya is a place of socialization and of stress alleviation. Here at Kinoya, the narrow space forces to relate to one another, under his/her unavoidable gaze. The design has the West and the East Asia beliefs about community spirit, closeness and brotherhood collide in a fun and joyful manner.

MATERIALS

hemlock and white spruce, reusing the furniture and lighting system from previous Kinoya.

05. Entrance inside the wood box
06. Bar and graffiti details
07. Bar
08. Wood pattern

Musashi Izakaya Restaurant

DESIGNER Vie Studio   **USE** Restaurant   **LOCATION** Sydney, Australia   **AREA** 150m²
PHOTOS Vie Studio

The renowned Musashi Izakaya Japanese Restaurant located at Haymarket, NSW has recently undergone a facelift to attract the young and adventurous. Vie Studio was engaged to take on this makeover project within a minimal budget and rebrand the restaurant with a strong oriental touch to echo the unique Japanese arts & culture.

The concept of Musashi bifurcated from the legendary Miyamoto Musashi, a swordsman and samurai who was the pioneer of the Dual Sword Technique. Exploring the idea of duality and designs of his costume, the story of this remarkable Japanese swordsman is brought to life on the restaurant walls with a vibrant twang of glamour.

The star of the restaurant is undeniably the magnificent artwork imprinted on plywood panels lining the wall, paying homage to Musashi's fortitude and bravery. Authentic Japanese patterns with heraldic texture and form are repeated throughout the restaurant, randomly found on customary banquet seats and on laser-cut motifs from the fascia to the feature wall within. The intense cultural expression, in contrast with the modern and contemporary approach, underlines its idiosyncrasy within the Sydney Chinatown neighborhood.

The yellow theme is deliberately applied to pop out from the heritage facade architecture and building that surround it; as well as to accentuate a fresh visual existence from its previous namesake. Following the trail of "freshness", timber veneer has been used in all furniture, joinery and decorative items to deliver a warm ambient to the entire space. The circular and triangular torqued silhouette pendant lights have become talk of the town, a reminiscence of a rich and fascinating literature from the Land of the Rising Sun.

MATERIALS
FSC plywood, timber veneer, Japanese floral print fabrics, lasercut panels, Jean Prouve Chairs, Prisma and Bellato wood veneer pendant lights

01. Significant drawing on the wall
02. Facade
03. Interior overview

04. Interior overview
05-06. Details

05

06

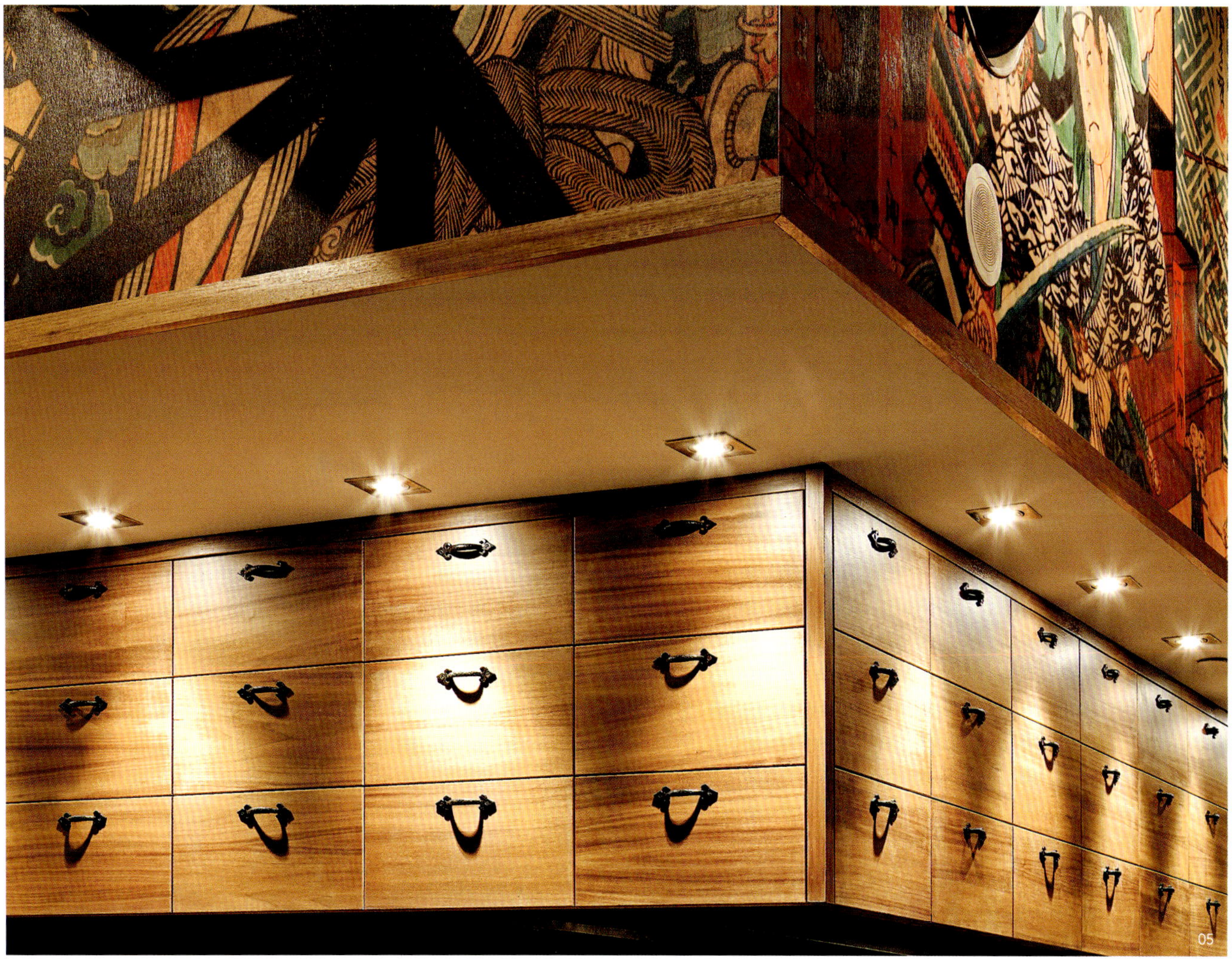

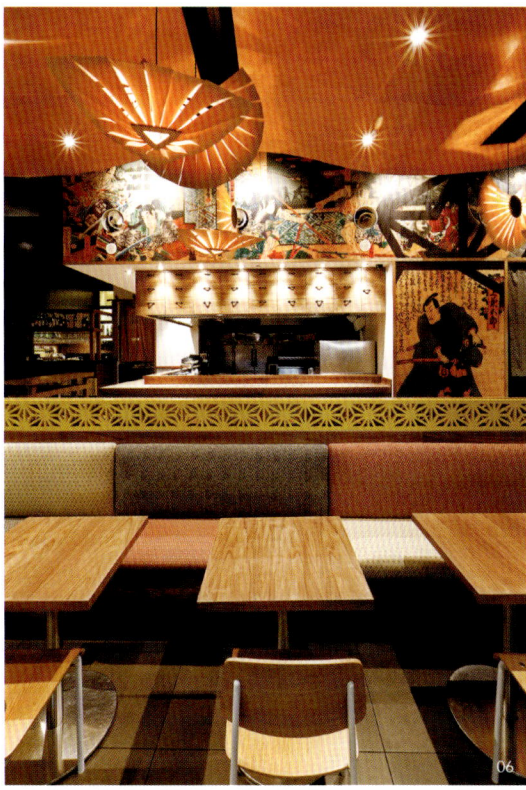

① Kitchen
② Drink Bar
③ Counter
④ Entry

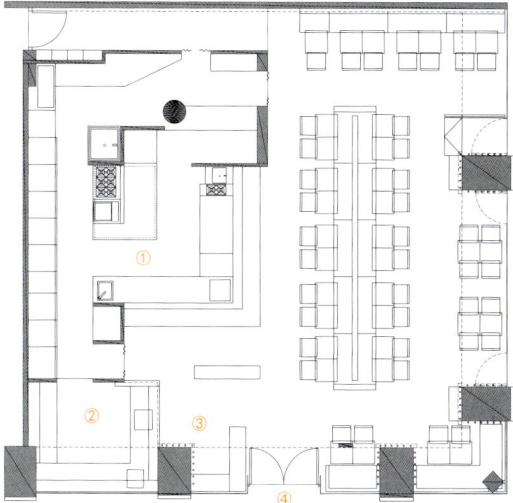

Plan

07-11. Details with Japanese culture characteristics

Saboten, Beijing

DESIGNER Aiji Inoue, Yuki Kanai/ DOYLE COLLECTION CO. LTD.   **USE** Restaurant   **LOCATION** Beijing, China   **CLIENT** Saboten Co., LTD.   **AREA** 346m²   **PHOTOGRAPHER** Satoru Umetsu / Nacasa & Partners Inc.

Deformation of our tradition and good localization are essential in order to make Japanese culture easier to be accepted by foreign countries. This is a Japanese cutlet restaurant chain called "Saboten", the first flagship restaurant in China. Here, viewing the future visions of restaurant chain, we made designs that will become useful manuals when expanding to China and also overseas.

First of all, one of our challenges was to grasp the right understanding of "Japanese images" that the foreigners prefer. We focused mainly on "traditional Japan". At present, compared with this modern style brand, effort is put into how to incorporate this "traditional Japan". One of our approaches was to add traditional aspects to the materials. Furthermore we made deformation and by adjusting this to modern style, we created a new identity. And this, in fact, made the foreigners easier to understand our outcome.

And here is another approach we challenged. We tried to understand the local culture and to partly localize the designs and layouts. People will see this from the height and position of the partitions. We also adopted round tables. This is one way of localization. Nevertheless, it is just one of our Japanese minds of hospitality known as "Omotenashi". We came up with this conclusion when we considered about improving customers satisfaction in a flexible way. But this does not mean that we created this Japanese restaurant so that it will look like Chinese restaurants.

In this way, Japanese restaurant Saboten that we "delivered" to China received a good reputation to a wide range of customers. And also to the Japanese, this restaurant gained attention with a fresh impression look. It has become an excellent example of integrating traditional Japan and contemporary Japan.

01. Full view of reception hall. Good balance motif that evokes feelings of Japan.
02. Overview of facade constructed with various elements. Horizontally long facade will not give a monotonous impression.
03. Ttsuboniwa, known as spot garden is located in the approach of the restaurant. This enables customers' feelings to shift toward the Japanese "wa" atmosphere.
04. In the center area of the customers' seats, there is a ceiling display with the Japanese "wa" motif which makes an impact on the whole seating. And over 30 evenly displayed pendant luminaries generate dignified atmosphere.

05. The center areas of the customers' seats are surrounded by partitions, displayed with folding screens in glass showcases. This area is the only place in the restaurant that is illuminated from the bottom. This amplifies surrounded images.
06. The floor of the innermost seats are placed one step higher so that customers will receive special feelings.
07. Each seating has different designs. All of these accumulations create the biggest identity to the whole restaurant design.

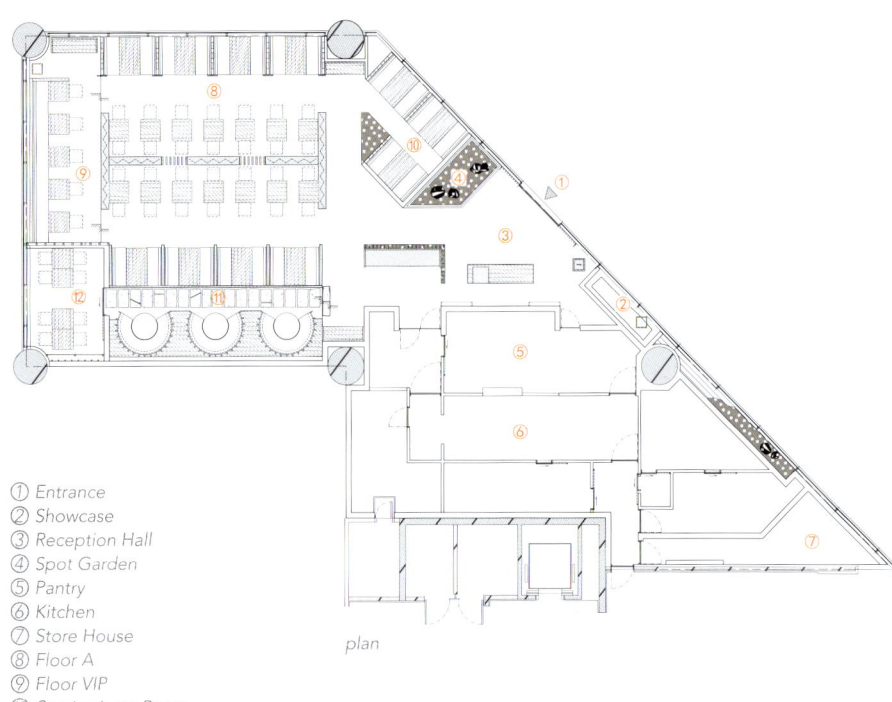

① Entrance
② Showcase
③ Reception Hall
④ Spot Garden
⑤ Pantry
⑥ Kitchen
⑦ Store House
⑧ Floor A
⑨ Floor VIP
⑩ Semi-private Room
⑪ Floor B
⑫ Private Room

plan

08. Detail of the wall surface attached with Kimono cloth. The wall surface can be seen through the strips that surround the round bench. These whole atmospheres emphasize the Japanese style more.
09. The booths are surrounded by reed screen (Japanese material called "Sudare") to enhance private feelings.
10. Though the restaurant is big, this is the only place where there is a wall. This wall is covered with many kinds of kimono cloth which bring traditional aspect to the whole restaurant.
11. There are openings between the booths' wall so that you do not have to feel oppression. Pendant luminaries will avoid eyes of the neighboring seats which will also give private feelings.

Elevation

Kemuri

DESIGNER PRISM DESIGN **USE** Restaurant / Bar **LOCATION** Shanghai, China **AREA** 200m²
PHOTOGRAPHER Nacasa & Partners Inc.

Using the title "Kemuri", literally meaning "smoke" in English, as main concept, the designer aims to express the willingness of offering the finest services as well as dining experiences that might be as misty as smoke, or as casual as sommelier. The main characteristics of "Kemuri" are the freshness of materials and the control of doneness during the cooking process. In order to preserve the original freshness and enjoy to a maximum the originality of the dish, only salt and peper has been used to minimize the artificial addition.
Illumination design follows this idea, using minimum lighting facilities to match the atmosphere of simple beauty. In fact, lighting facilities provided by "NVC" present a color temperature of 2700k, under which the food can be felt most deliciously both in visual perception and psychology.
The anticipation of the owner was to show a specific Asia worldview to be recognized by people abroad, as presented in the film "Kill Bill", combined with a representation of smoke with design approach. The whole external windows facade is lighting in red, which is the national color of both China and Japan, symbolizing the willing of culture interaction between 2 countries. Considering the balance of ecologic aspect and visual effect, the whole illumination system uses LED products. The opening time covers all periods of solar illumination. Therefore the lighting project has been also designed to match this natural evolution of sunshine.
When observing smoke, we discovered that its presentation of cloud-like form is composed by multiples changing lines and their intercourse. So we interpreted "kemuri" as a 3D constitution, which has been shaped by continue of lines as our main element.

We used hemp ropes to express the idea of "line". The strength comes from thousands of thin hemps. The owner picked hemp rope, as he takes human relationship as mutual aid into consideration. The other reason comes from traditional Japanese architectures, which also relates to illumination project. One of the important aims is the representation of hemp ropes' silhouette and shadow.
Illumination planning of dining space focuses on showing the shapes of ropes in various ways, accompanied with 2700K LED spotlights and their freely movable electricity rails. This configuration aims to highlight the natural unevenness of mortar wall. Besides, to avoid the straight light, a piece of grading cover has been used to create soft and nature lighting atmosphere, as we have seen the scene of sunshine filtering through foliage in traditional architecture.
Counter is a cooking place for owner's "self-performance". This stage located at not only in the center of restaurant, but also at the most prominent place with the highest illumination, as it asked for spotlights-like effects for "actor". Special seats taking bell clock as its motif enhanced the 3D structure. There are LED spotlights at flooring and ceiling lever, to create a floating mirage.
Tatami room has been designed in a different way. The much lighter atmosphere isolated the space from the outside Japanese garden of red fantasy, which hovering red fireflies. Illumination planning that only oriented by LED tapes light and pendant lighting support the performance of atmosphere in traditional landscape.

MATERIALS
mortar, scrap wood, wood floor, red film sheet, aging steel object, hemp rope, ceramic plate art, bambo landscape, stainless steel

01. The movie "Kill Bill" film work gives a performance with a strong conflict. External performance of facade window glass faces national color of China and Japan "red", intending to reflect the theme of "Kill Bill" movies.
02. The live stage of cooking human, illumination has set the highest in the store.

03

04

03. Japanese architecture expression in the silhouette of the rope.
04. To achieve both functionality and art
05-06. The most impressive color in the restaurant is red.

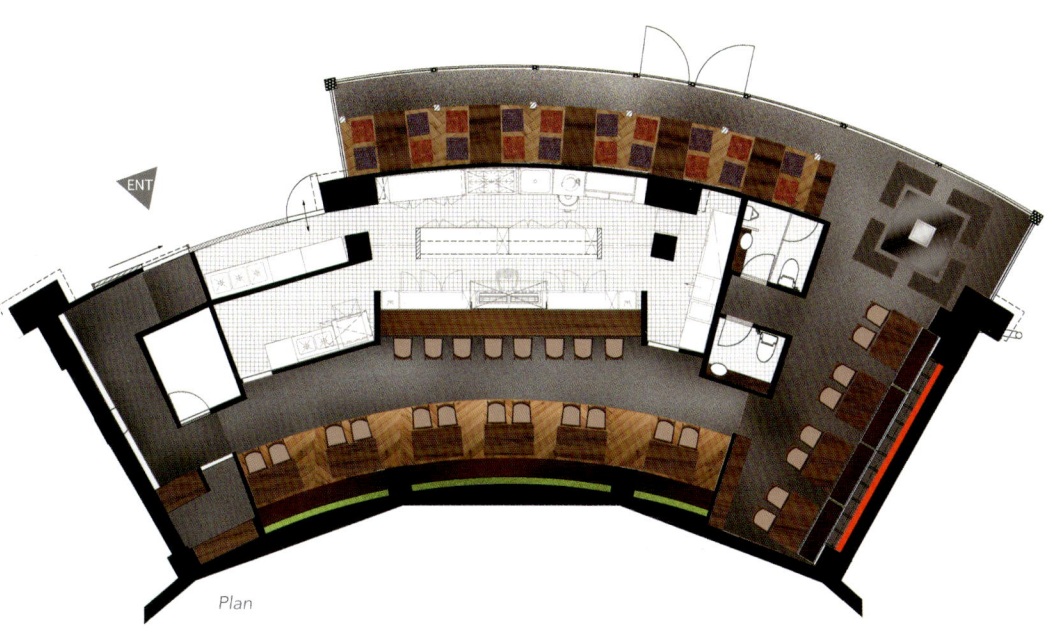

Plan

07. Tatami room is a garden of red fantastic. The appearance of inside and outside space is different.
08. The theme of shrines and temples of Japanese architecture.
09. Interior details.

08

09

161

Sushizilla

DESIGNER Vie Studio **USE** Restaurant **LOCATION** Sydney, Australia **CLIENT** Sushizilla **AREA** 202m² **PHOTOGRAPHER** Andrew Worssam

With "Bringing back the fun mojo of a kaiten restaurant with exceptional food quality" as Sushizilla's mission, this beast of a sushi train restaurant draws references from Japanese comics and pop culture. Situated within the Central Park development, Sushizilla Restaurant and Sushizilla Express's vibrant interior adds a fun-loving personality to the Chippendale Creative Precinct.

Pushing the boundaries of traditional sushi train restaurant, Sushizilla offers touch screen ordering system for each patron apart from sushi available on the train. While for people on the go, Sushizilla Express offers self-serve takeaway service within a walk-in kiosk.

At first glance, the neon sign, the splashes of color and tetris-like linear geometry teleports you into the digital world of an old-school gaming arcade. Vie Studio focuses on creating an engaging shop front facade to the restaurant as a response to the client's brief in providing a unique dining experience.

The interior pays tribute to early computer games raster graphic through the ingenious use of rectilinear geometry exhibited in the colored square tiles and milk crates.

Sushizilla's energetic color scheme is beautifully balanced by the subtlety of neutral engineered stone, textured paint finish and exposed concrete. The contrast between vibrancy and neutral tones adds a playful contemporary twist to the once-hip gaming arcade.

The overall design is complemented by the black and white comical mural, which is the canvas of Siori Kitajima, the talented artist.

MATERIALS
steel, milk crate, metal mesh, engineered stone, colored tiles, exposed concrete, neon sign

01-02. Facade
03-05. Interior space

06-09. Interior details
10. Comical mural on the wall

09

Plan

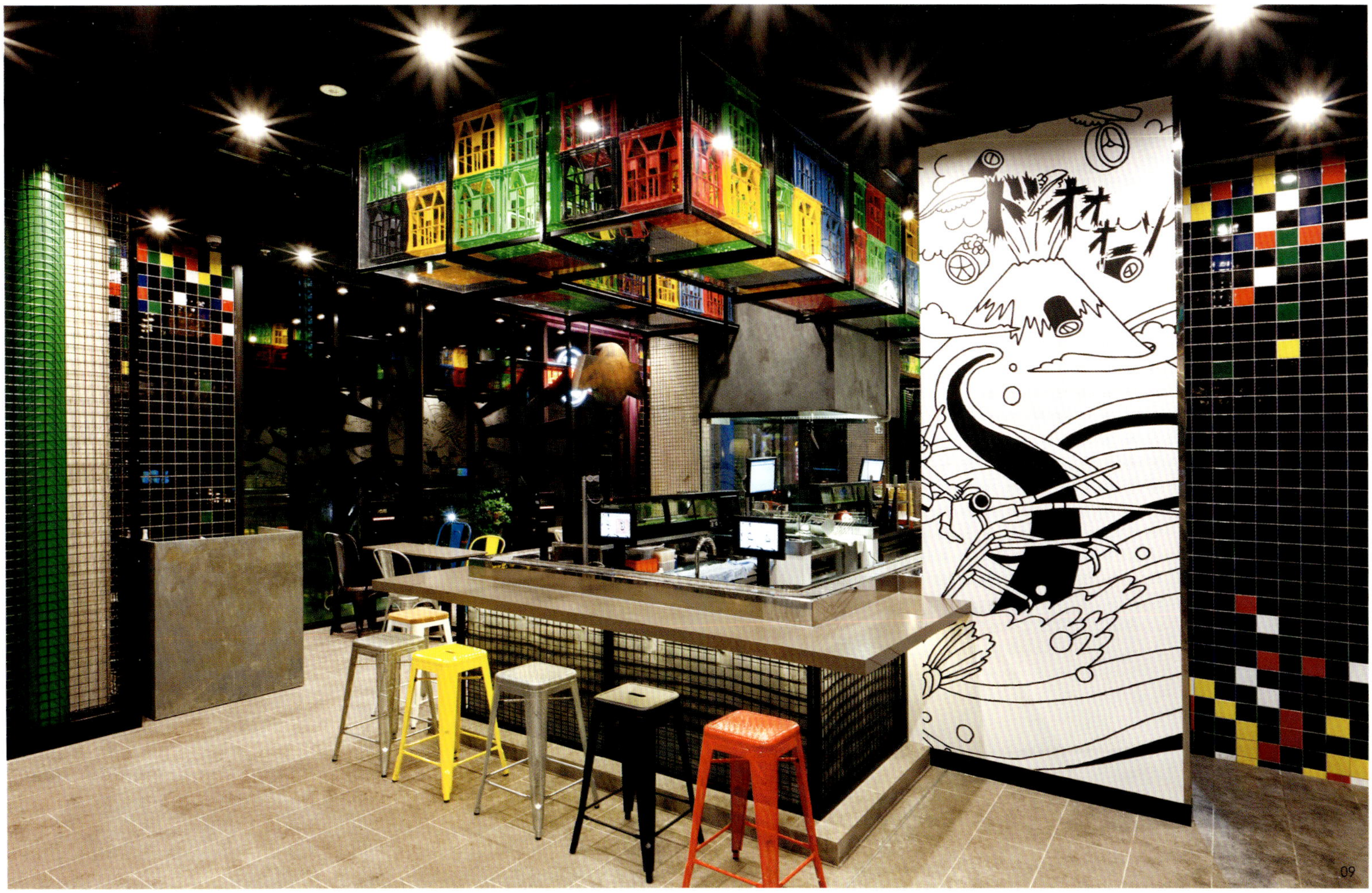

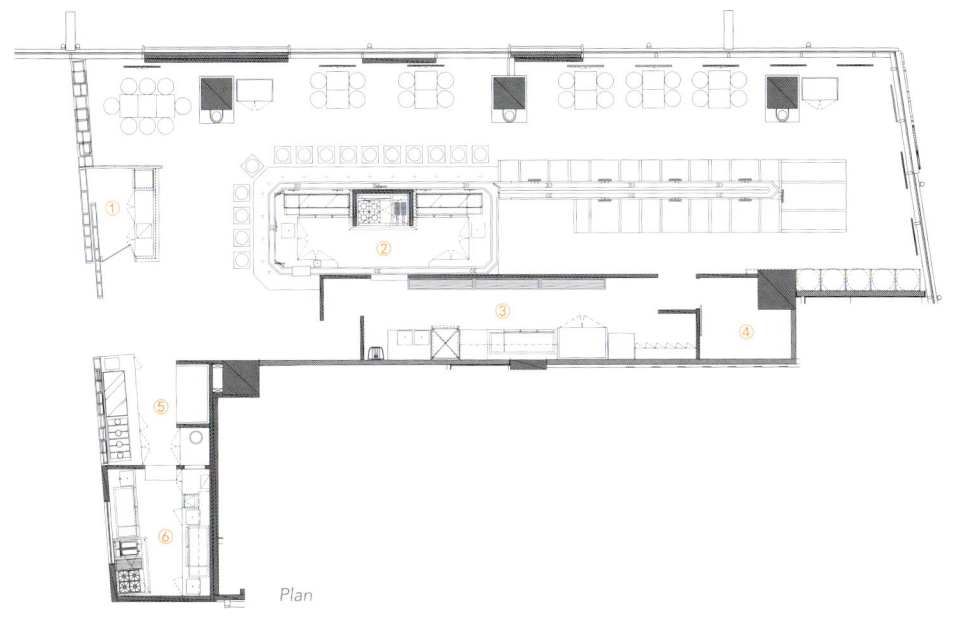

① Cashier
② Sushi Prep Area
③ Washing Area
④ Store Room
⑤ Self-service Area
⑥ Prep Area

10

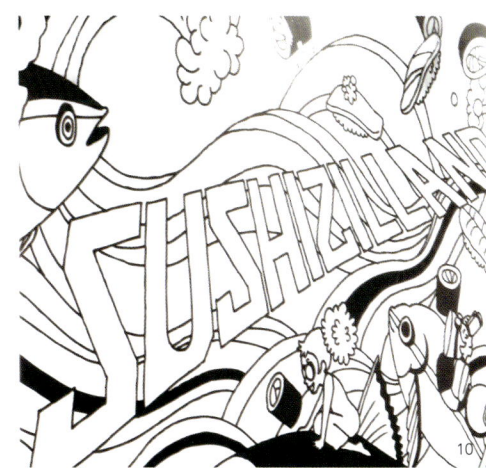

11-13. Colorful milk crates

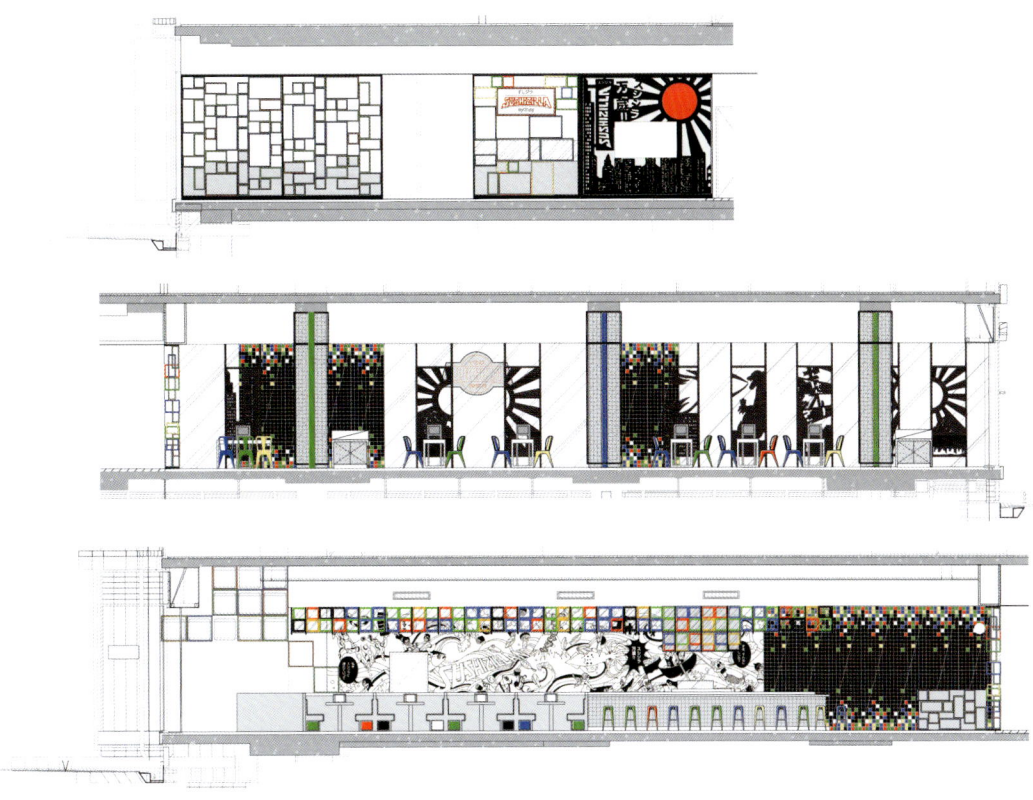

Elevations

The Pasta & Grill's

DESIGNER design office Dress Inc.　**USE** Restaurant / Bar　**LOCATION** Osaka, Japan　**AREA** 60m²
PHOTOGRAPHER Nacása & Partners Inc.

The Pasta & Grill's is located in Tenma Osaka, Japan. Various local restaurants and bars are dotted around this area. As the name tells, it serves tasty pastas and grilled beef.

We tried to create the restaurant that looks like existing at the place long time. Painted brick-like wall and the use of antique tiles make us feel its history. By using the stripe patterns for some elements of the interiors, such as tent on the facade, fabrics for chairs etc., we give the sense of urbaneness to the space. People who come to the restaurant experience the warm and relaxed atmosphere by all those elements of the restaurant.

We also works for its Logo and Visuals such as business card and the invitations. For Logo, we show their spirits of the teamwork for cooking by using the icon of the cap meaning "we are team!" And for invitation card, we focused on their fresh dishes to make visitors feel "I want to go eat there!" by showing the various fresh materials used for cooking such as pasta, vegetables, fruits, bread and so on. We hope we created the good experience for visitors with all the designs.

01. Interior view
02. Facade
03. Entrance
04. Interior

05-06. Interior overview
07. The view from the exterior

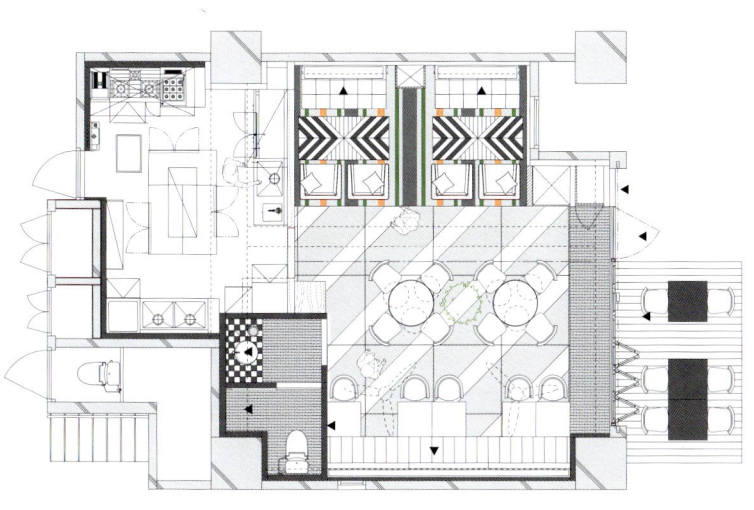

Plan

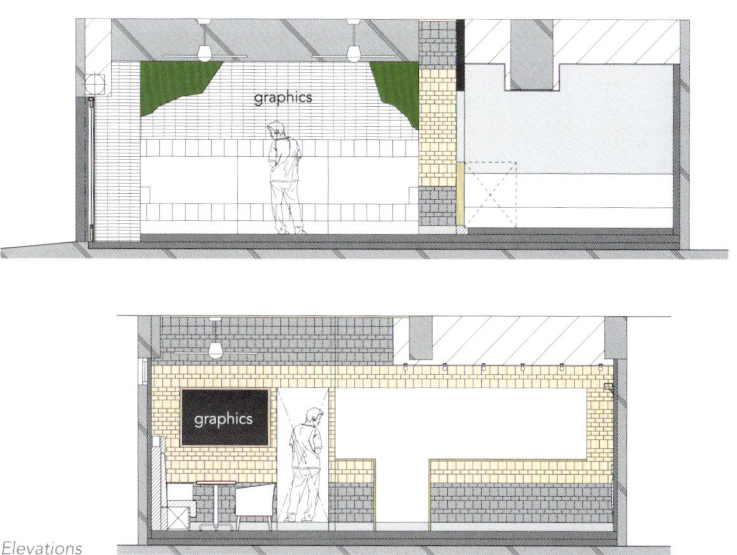

Elevations

BARBARESCO

DESIGNER Aiji Inoue, Yoshito Nakahara / DOYLE COLLECTION co. ltd.   **USE** Restaurant   **LOCATION** Hachinohe-shi, Aomori, Japan   **AREA** 81m2   **CLIENT** GMKBros Inc.   **PHOTOGRAPHER** Satoru Umetsu / Nacasa & Partners Inc.

"BARBARESCO" is a trattoria enjoying the assortment style of casual Italian dishes and selected wines by the sommelier. It is basically arranged with color schemes emphasizing "exquisite restaurant" and stressing the designs of softness for casual usage.

We have spent an adequate time for the layout, and planned deliberately for the convenience and dramatic impact, one of which is, the entrance. A murky passage is secured by the flow plan reversing the escape route and the entrance originally set for this tenant. Moreover, the first place you step in is where wine cellar stands in rows, creating feeling of surprise as if entering from the back door. Also, one of the feature is that the chef's and sommelier's stages (kitchen and drink counter) have been separated to clearly emphasize the management style. The guests may choose the zone according to the number of people and usage. Furthermore, matching each zone with characteristic pendant light, will produce unique and dimensional effect.

The window shade gives the entire sense of unity to the main hall. This is a design with randomly piled up alphabets, "b.a.r.b.a.r.e.s.c.o". This custom-designed window shade has functional design showing glimpses of restaurant and attracting people's interests from outside, while obtaining sense of security inside, and free from glances outside. A lot of graphic patterns are used and the balance of figures and ground are examined carefully.

VIP room is designed with unified taste inside the restaurant, with gradually upgraded details to obtain feeling of high-quality-sense for the VIPs. The characteristic pendant light hung here is designed from the inspiration of wine's raw material "grape".

04

05

01. The entrance lies ahead, walking through this murky passage. To make an impressive passage, the ceiling is built in a vault type and the illumination is set dimly.
02. The logo is marked on the wall. "Grape" motif is designed.
03. The tables and seats for the guests are mainly divided into three zones.
04. A view of the restaurant inside from the back.
05. Take a first step in and you will see drink counter. The sommelier welcomes you.

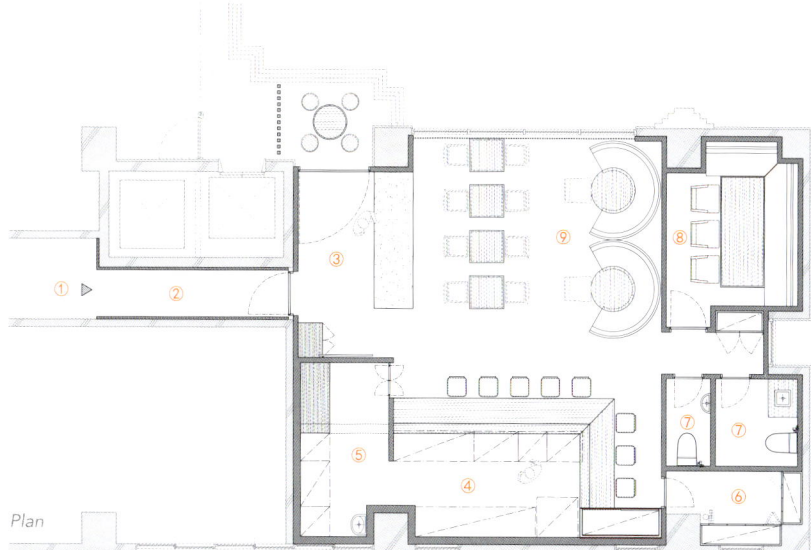

① Entrance
② Passage
③ Beverage Counter
④ Open kitchen
⑤ Kitchen
⑥ Store House
⑦ WC
⑧ VIP room
⑨ Main floor

Plan

06. The counter seats.
07. The custom-designed window shades with randomly piled alphabets of this restaurant's name are set at the left section in the back.
08. VIP room. The techniques are used in places to make the room look broader.
09. Up above the round sofa seat, the labels of wine provided at the restaurant are hung on Zettel 'z A5, which Ingo Maurer designed.

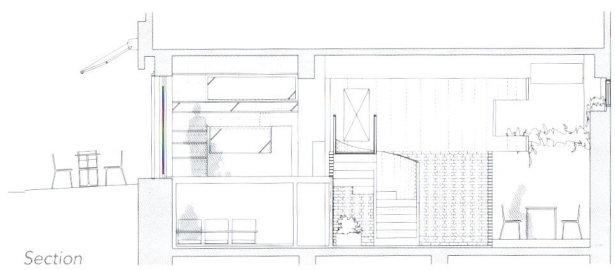
Section

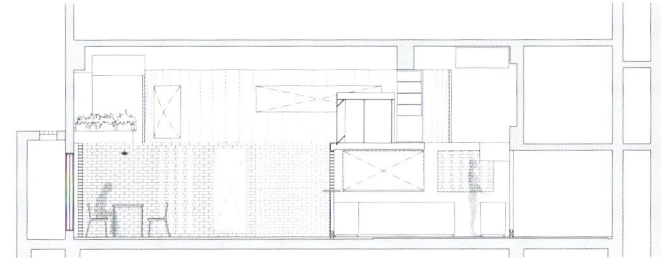

+green

DESIGNER Chikara Ohno / sinato   **USE** Restaurant / Shop   **LOCATION** Tokyo, Japan   **AREA** 111.53m²   **CLIENT** Dream Studio Co., Ltd.   **PHOTOGRAPHER** Toshiyuki Yano

This project is for an organic restaurant on Jiyu Street, which is only a short walk from Komazawa Olympic Park, one of the largest parks in Tokyo. The restaurant is on the ground floor of a three story apartment building and is a half level underground.

The restaurant has three basic functions: a takeout bistro, an organic food shop and a restaurant. The most distinctive feature of the premises lies in its floor level, which is 1.61m below the ground level of the entrance. This means that the interior ceiling height is 4.39m.

The starting point of our design was to study the arrangement of the three functions in such a volume. By placing the restaurant on the half underground floor, the takeout counter at the front entrance at ground level and the shop shifting diagonally away from the takeout counter, we could allow light into the restaurant area from the facade aperture above. The shop space is 0.56m higher than the takeout space as the kitchen fits beneath it.

There are three floor levels for each function, so people move up and down through the space. We created different walls in the upper and lower spaces, partitioning the space in different ways so that people can experience different circumstances and be curious about the other spaces.

01-02. Interior
03. Overview of facade
04. Even below grade level the dining space receives ample natural light.

In the upper space, a white wall hide the original wall and equipment like air conditioning systems and piping. The wall also serves as a frame which emphasizes the graphics, plants or interior scenery of the restaurant. This wall surrounds the stairs and delineates a large void in the interior of the space. In the lower space, you can still sense the form of the white wall floating above your head, which is quite different from the plan of the restaurant floor which is partitioned by brick wall. The brick wall turns at a right angle many times, creating hall space on the inside. It also forms a private room, kitchen and storeroom on the outside between the brick wall and the original wall. The hall space is divided into three places but at the same time they connected. We distributed small plantings so that they would be visible from anywhere in the interior.

MATERIALS
floor mortar (skeleton), wooden flooring
wall brick, painting (white), concrete (skeleton)
ceiling concrete (skeleton)

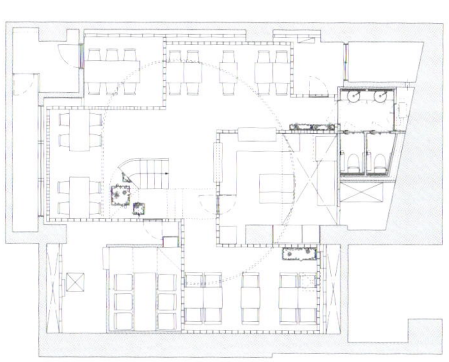

Lower Floor Plan

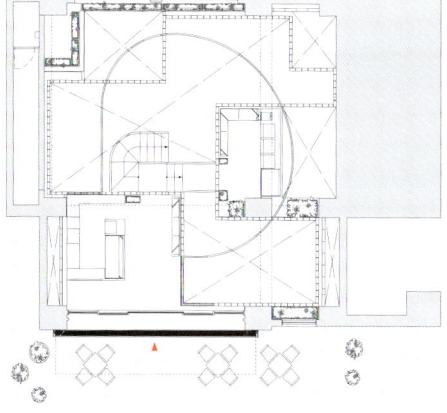

Upper Floor Plan

Usually, we divide the space in one way.

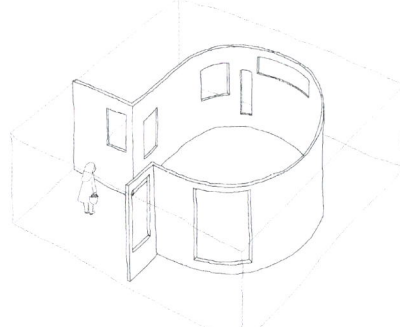

Divide the space by curved line

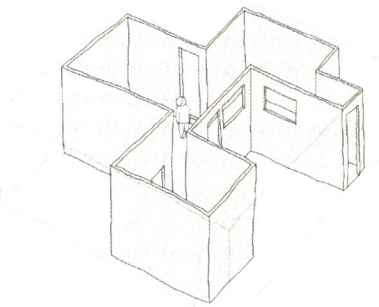

Divide the space by zigzag line

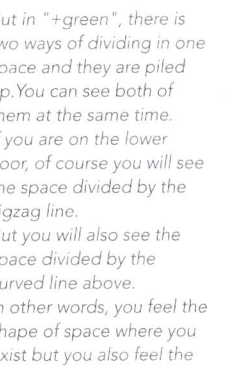

But in "+green", there is two ways of dividing in one space and they are piled up. You can see both of them at the same time. If you are on the lower floor, of course you will see the space divided by the zigzag line.
But you will also see the space divided by the curved line above.
In other words, you feel the shape of space where you exist but you also feel the shape of space where you don't exist.

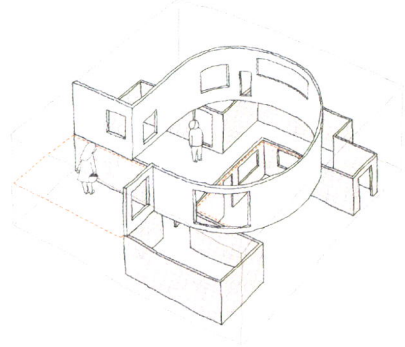

05. Interior
06. The curved wall above links all the spaces below.
07. The zig-zag wall allows for a variety of dining spaces with different levels of privacy.

08-09. Interior
10. The sweeping curved wall at ground level gives the feeling of a wide space with real depth.

Tokyo Baby Cafe

DESIGNER nendo **USE** Cafe **LOCATION** Tokyo, Japan **PHOTOGRAPHER** Jimmy Cohrssen

The design for a "parent and child cafe" on Tokyo's Omotesando, is for parents to enjoy being out with small children without worrying about the issues around them. The cafe is fully stocked with picture books and toys, including a playroom, private rooms and separate spaces for nursing and changing diapers. Wide aisles make it easy to move around with a stroller, and light switches and door handles are placed high up to keep children away from them.
The cafe is designed to be enjoyed by two very different sizes of users, "parents" and "small children", so the interior design plays on the difference in scale. The parents and the children see the world through different eyes. Take a table as the example: adults live their lives being aware of tabletops, and the things placed on top of them. But children see the underside of the table. The table legs may look like pillars, and the reverse of the tabletop is like a roof. The cafe's "absolutely huge" and "absolutely tiny" furnishings take advantage of these two perspectives, one for the adult and the other for the children.

A nursing sofa becomes a playroom when blown up on a massive scale, and a diaper changing table when shrunk to minuscule proportions. Big windows pair with small ones, and so do the big light bulbs. The floorboards vary in size, and the undersides of tables, where parents eyes don't reach, hide pictures of parent and baby animals. As a matter of fact, the theme of "parents and children" can be found all around the Tokyo Baby cafe, always ready for their parent and child visitors.

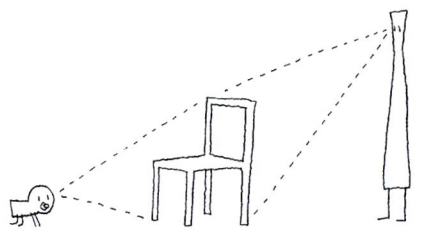

Sketch

01. Interior overview
02-03. Details
04. Interior overview

05-08. Interior details

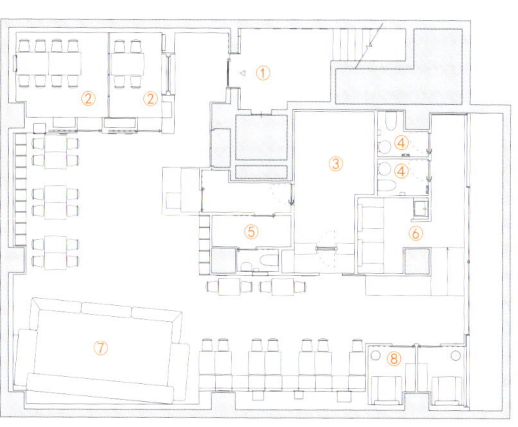

Plan

① Entrance
② Private Room
③ Kitchen
④ WC
⑤ Office
⑥ Diaper-changing Area
⑦ Play Area
⑧ Nursing Room

01. Interior overview
02. Entrance of the restarant
03. Interior wall feature
04. Counter

Café & Meal MUJI, Chengdu

DESIGNER Takashi Sugimoto / Super Potato **USE** Cafe / Restaurant **LOCATION** Chengdu, China
CLIENT MUJI **PHOTOGRAPHER** MUJI, Chengdu Flagship Store

Japanese retailer MUJI has opened its largest overseas store in China on December 12, 2014 with a grand opening in emerging fashion and retail city Chengdu, marking its 100th store in the mainland of China. The new MUJI flagship store sits inside Sino-Ocean Taikoo Li Mall, walking distance to Chengdu's hottest shopping district Chun Xi Road. Designed by Japanese interior designer Takashi Sugimoto, this 3,141m^2, four-storey space hosts everyday objects reflective of MUJI's concept while still maintaining Chinese characteristics in a more refreshing way.

The Chengdu concept store represents a number of firsts for Chinese consumers and MUJI. It boasts the first Café & Meal MUJI on the third floor and is dedicated to locally sourced goods such as rice from Northeast China, lemon from An Yue, Sichuan, and Pu'er tea from Yunnan Province.

05. Dining area
06. Outdoor seats
07-08. Interior details

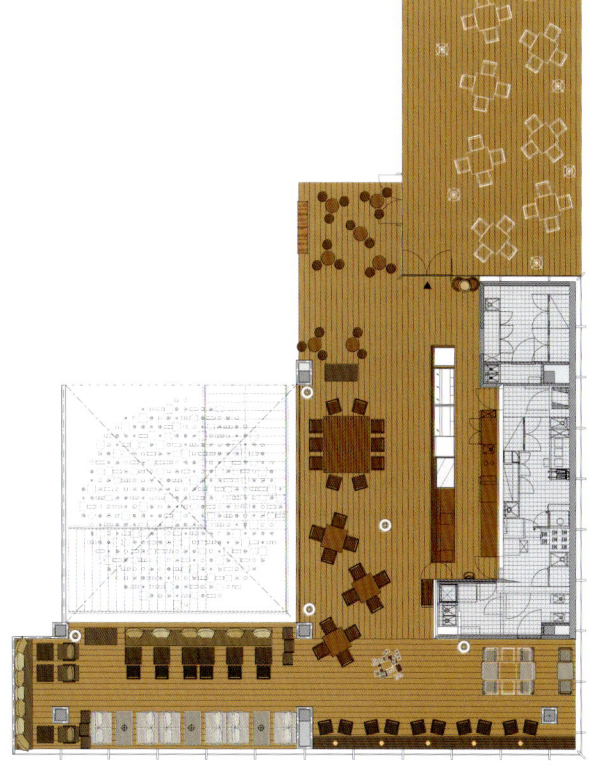

Plan

01-02. Entrance
03. Interior
04. Outdoor view

Kotokoto Dining

DESIGNER Naoya Matsumoto Design   **USE** College cafeteria   **LOCATION** Otsu-shi, Shiga, Japan
AREA 520m²   **PHOTOGRAPHER** Takeshi Asano

This design is the modification of a school canteen. More than 200 students will use this canteen during the lunch breaks. The designer views the space as a "flexible" one, for a party, a bazaar, or a lecture, etc. All required functions are expressed in the space.

For instance, a bold kitchen and DJ both are established in the section which is used for the party. Also, the section for people gathering is made for a forum or conference. The old school canteen turns out to be a communication space.

05-07. Interior details

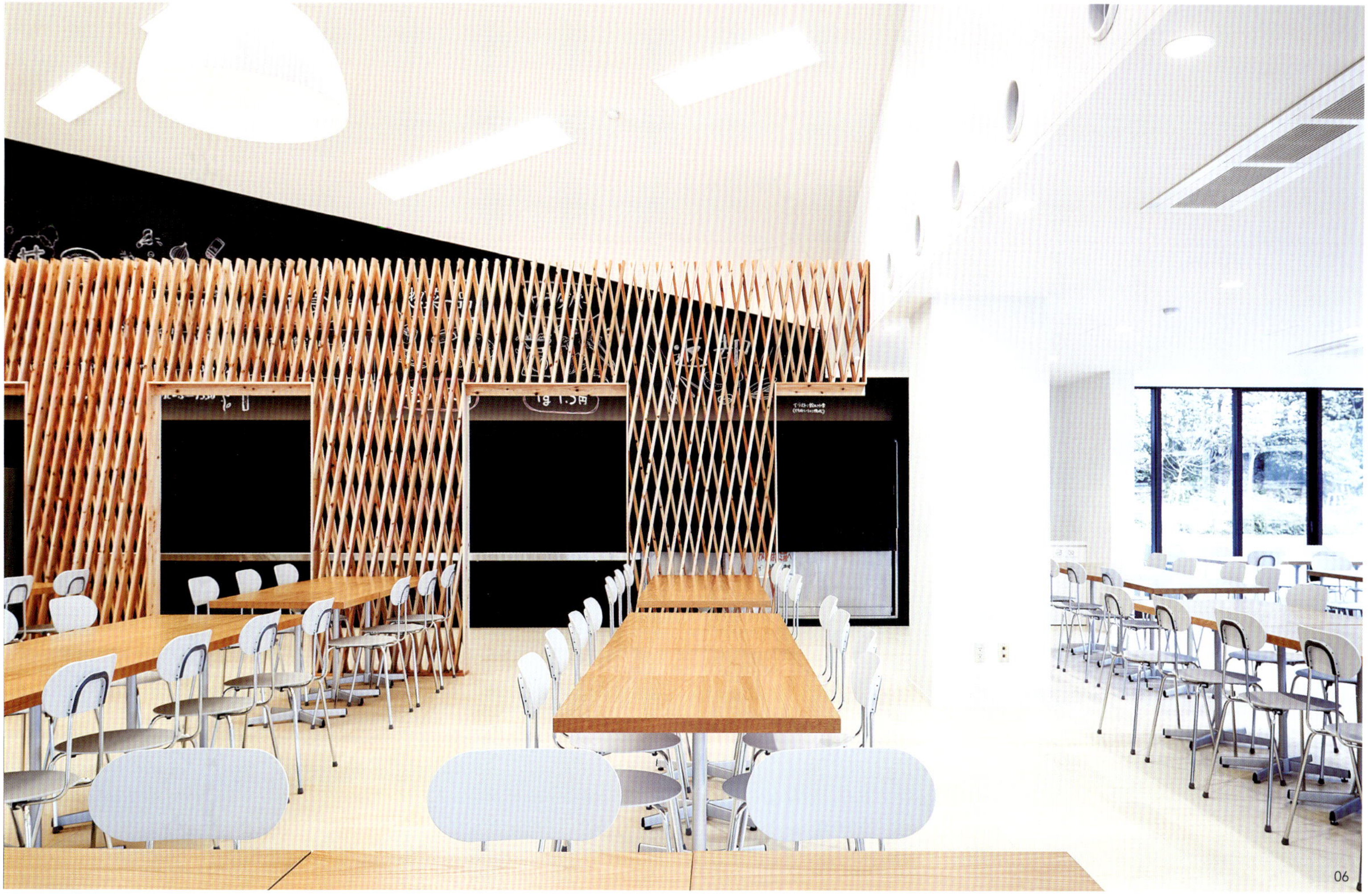

08

09

09-11. Interior views

01. Branch detail
02. Graphic tools
03. Sketch
04. Facade
05. Interior
06. Counter table
07. Interior

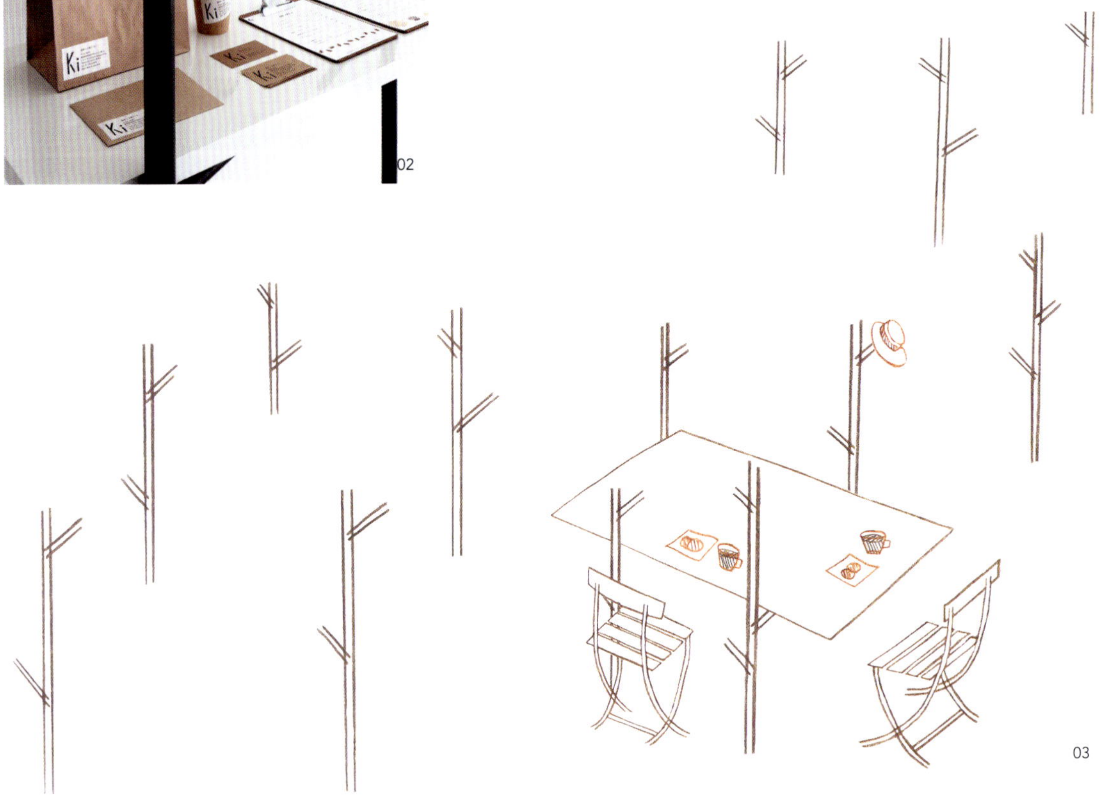

Cafe Ki

DESIGNER Seiji Oguri, Yohei Oki / id inc. **USE** Cafe **LOCATION** Tokyo, Japan **CLIENT** Cafe Ki / Mametora Kashiten **PHOTOS** id inc.

Cafe Ki opened in Setagaya-ku, Tokyo in Japan, which was designed by Japanese design office id. Ki means a tree in Japanese. It is a cafe where coffee and pastries can be enjoyed in a space like a yard or a forest. The pure white space enhances the coffee colored trees.

The "tree" standing inside the cafe takes a role as a steel table leg. Hats and coats can be hung on the highly extended table legs.

Although a large number of people can sit around the big table, it can maintain a sense of comfortable distance while sharing the table with a different group since wooden branches help to divide the space on the table. Moreover, the leg of the table randomly stands and those who sit down can freely choose a place to sit.

Japanese design office id designed for Cafe Ki not only the interior but also, the graphics, costumes, website, original products, and etc.

Materials
table legs steel / espresso color painted finish
table top wood / white painted finish
wall wall paper / white painted finish
floor wood / white painted finish

① Kitchen
② Cafe Space
③ Entrance

Floor Plan

Interior Elevation A

Interior Elevation B

Interior Elevation C

Interior Elevation D

Table

Counter Table

08-10. Interior
11. Sugar tray of the leaf motif

Restaurant Izaki

DESIGNER andfujiizaki **USE** Restaurant **LOCATION** Kashiwa, Japan **AREA** 22.65m²
PHOTOGRAPHER Taku Hata

This 52 years old wooden building stands on a triangular plot. The space of the first floor was converted and rebuilt into a new restaurant.

The cuts of 200 years old Oregon pine are the main elements for the interior design. The annual rings of each piece of wood are the metaphor of our respect towards the owners' long career in culinary arts.

The facade towards the street has a 9m wide opening which consists of sliding doors. Therefore customers can move freely in and out of the building and also use the street as a part of passage. The counter table is made by joint pieces of Oregon pine. Each seat is made out of a solid piece of timber. In the dining area there is space for 10 seats and tables. Each table is 70cm in width. The last table has a raised floored seating which is more convenient for customers with accompanying children.

The kitchen is openly viewed from the counter table. Field of view is carefully controlled by the floor level. It enables the customer to see the cooking process and enjoy conversations with the chef. It also allows the chef to be more aware of what is happening on the outside and being able to make contact with people passing by.

Each unique tile for the walls or wooden materials for fitting and flooring are made out of individual pieces. However, the tones of color are limited. The warm color of wood becomes the main element in making this intimate space. The reconstruction of the damaged main structure was repaired and reinforced with quake resisting walls and hardware.

01. Facade
02-04. Interior space

① Back Space
② Kitchen
③ Bench
④ Seat
⑤ WC
Plan

05

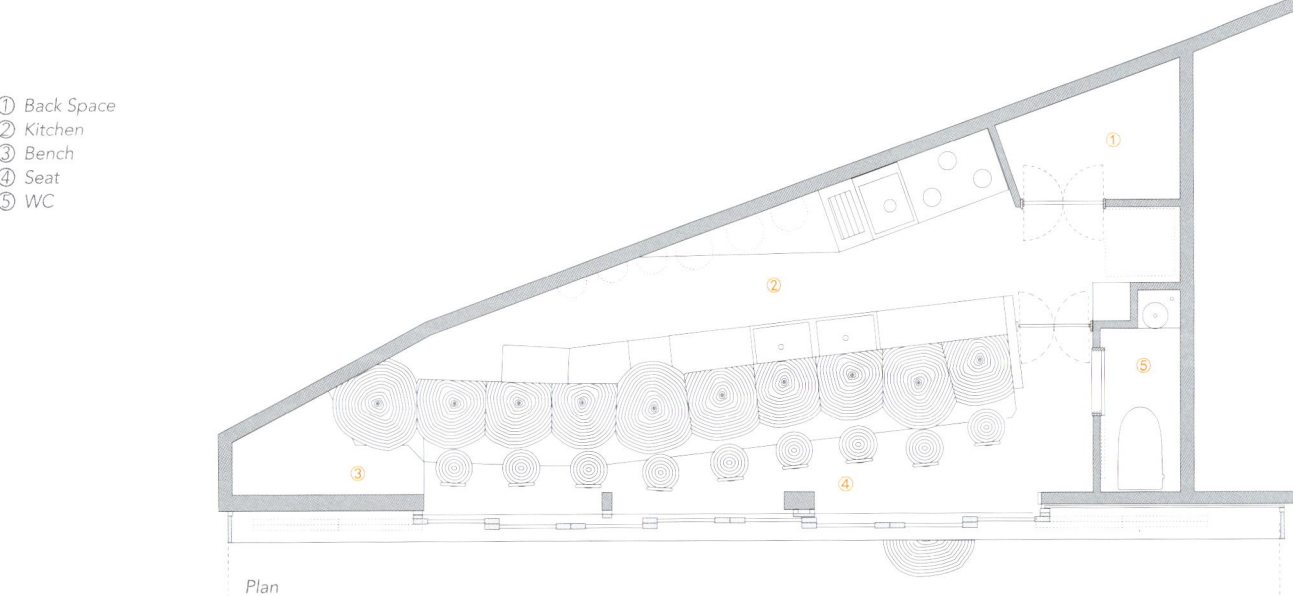

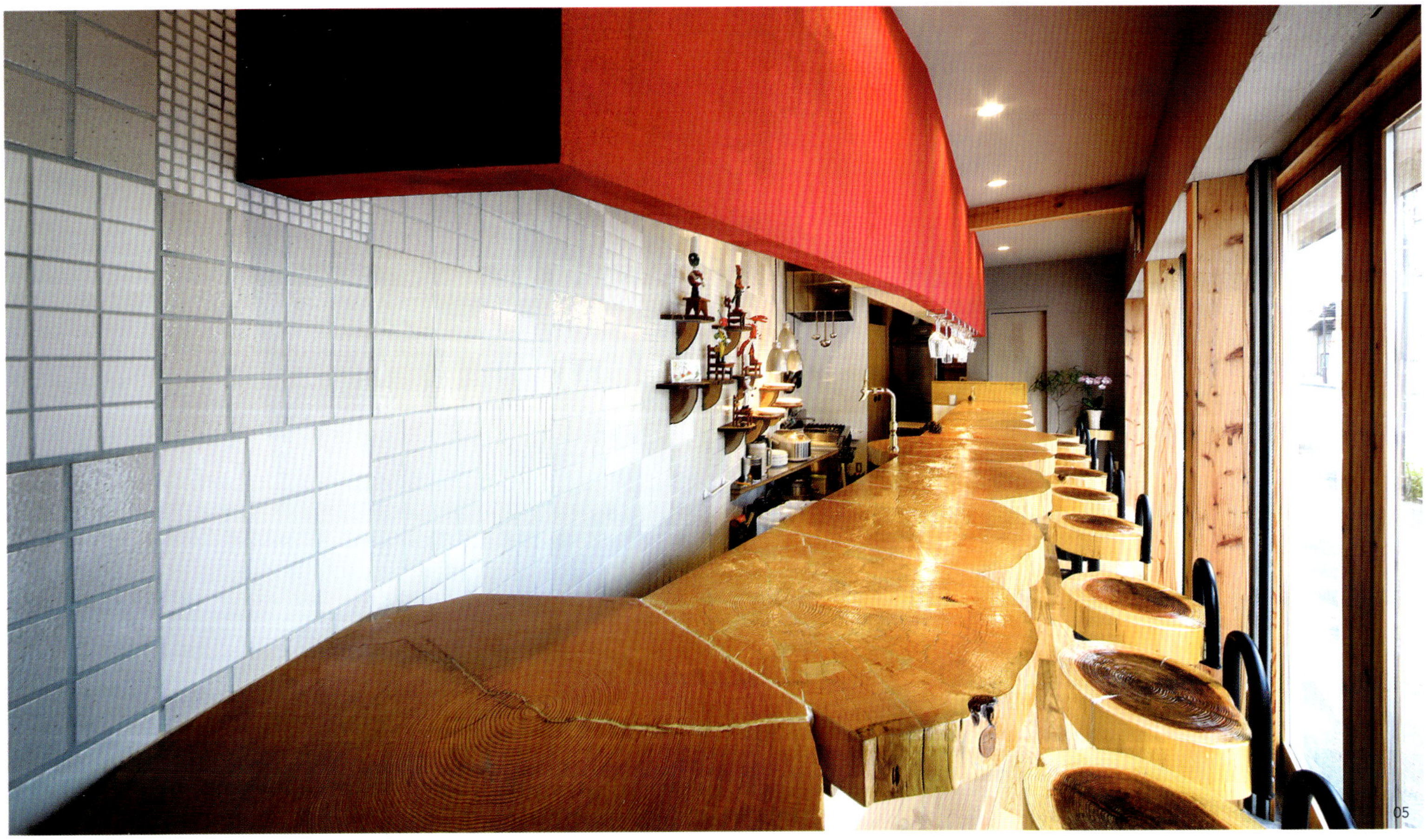

05. Interior overview
06-08. Interior details

① Restroom for Men
② Restroom for Women
③ Kitchen
④ Table Seat
⑤ Reception
⑥ Staff Room
⑦ Cloak Room
⑧ Shower Room
⑨ Wash Room for Staff

Plan

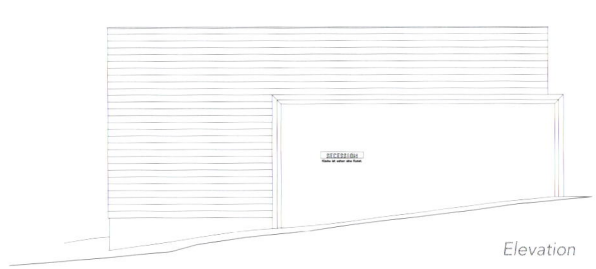

Elevation

Secession

DESIGNER PROCESS5 DESIGN Co.,Ltd. **USE** Restaurant **LOCATION** Tanabe-city, Wakayama, Japan
AREA 99.60m² **PHOTOGRAPHER** Stirling Elmendorf

This is a new construction plan of a restaurant in Tanabe City located in Wakayama Prefecture. The owner and chef is an art lover, and he particularly respective the Vienna Secession with respect to art. While designing the restaurant, he frequently talked about art apart from Cuisine. Therefore we came up with a plan for realizing the global outlook of the owner. The concept that we came up with is "Dinner party that turns into art". Painting, sculpture, among others, are often mentioned as art; however, there are few occasions of describing food as an art, which is extremely important for people.
In this restaurant, one dish of food, and every single scene such as scene of having food and scene of providing service is trimmed and put in one picture, creating a space where these scenes become an art.
Fusion of one dish, joyful conversation of customers, and graceful service is certainly apt to be called an art, and along with several Vienna Secession pictures displayed in the restaurant, they render an excellent time for dinner party. The owner chef named this restaurant SECESSION, which means Vienna Secession, the art movement. On the facade of the restaurant, we have put the following line in German: "Cooking is still an art"

01. Entrance
02. Facade
03-04. Interior

05-07. Interior with art pieces

Bluberi Stonebridge

DESIGNER emmanuelle moureaux   **USE** Frozen Yogurt Store   **LOCATION** Woodbridge, USA
AREA 68m²

Bluberi is a health-conscious frozen yoghurt brand founded in Washington, DC. As a result of the brand's expansion, we were commissioned to handle the design of the store's concept and the interior scheme of Bluberi's second shop, located in Stonebridge, Virginia.
In line with the basic "delicious, fun, and healthy" theme, we decided to project an image of the brand that would be memorable and far-reaching, in line with Blueberi's future expansion plans.

The interior of the shop features an image of a blueberry tree with its strong branches extending outwards, seemingly bursting with energy and laden with juicy blueberries in 13 colors – the fruit for which the store is named. We also selected lighting fixtures and furniture that call to mind the round, plump shape of the fruit, giving the whole interior a cohesive look.

In keeping with the image of a frozen yoghurt store that uses only non-fat, healthy ingredients, we made special efforts to select appropriate materials for the interior, opting for only translucent colors and Benjamin Moore paints that contain no harmful organic components, for instance.

Blueberry tree motifs were also used for the store's website, cards and other promotional materials, and the colors of the logos were changed according to the spatial design of certain areas. Collectively, these details helped to create a total brand image for our client. The result was a store that aptly reflected the ideals of Bluberi's young, 29-year-old husband-and-wife owners.

MATERIALS
floor   tile
wall   AEP paint
ceiling   AEP paint

01. Interior overview
02. Facade
03-05. Interior details

① Customer Area
② Service Area
③ Prep Kitchen
④ Storage
⑤ Office

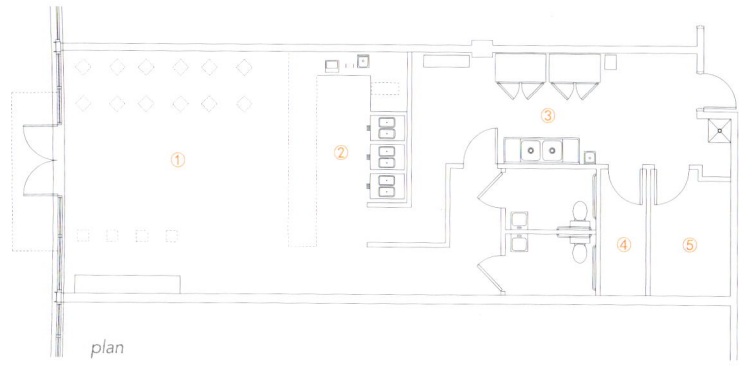

plan

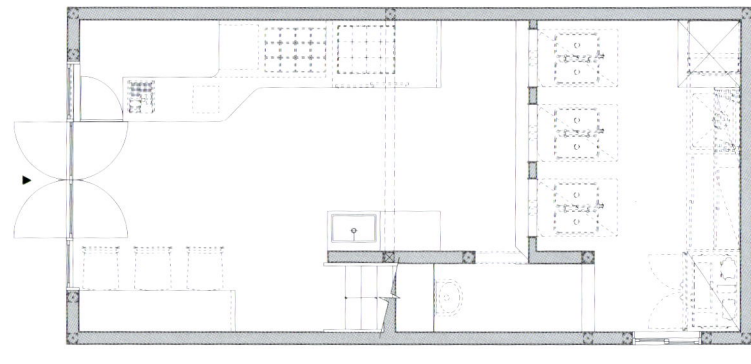

Lani Yogurt

DESIGNER Yasuhiro Sone **USE** Yogurt bar / Shop **LOCATION** Yokohama, Japan
PHOTOGRAPHER Hideo Mori / amano studio

This project is the design of Lani Yogurt, a self-serve frozen yogurt bar / shop in Chinatown, Yokohama. The owner of Lani Yogurt spent three years creating an original recipe for frozen yogurt that has a rich flavor and a refreshing taste. In the shop, customers can enjoy choosing their own flavor of yogurt, size of serving, and toppings.

The designer's most important task was to create a space that would allow tourists to get to know the shop and experience the taste of the yogurt. Accordingly, at first, the designer designed the logo is the cute and catchy icon of the shop. The logo is also printed on the yogurt cups. As customers walk through the store, and eat their yogurt through the Chinatown area, the cups act as a walking advertisement.

The interior of the shop features shades of pink and brown, coordinating with the logo. By using the building's characteristic that is the long and narrow, the designer placed the kitchen and backyard the inmost space. The layout of the shop leads customers around the shop while they choose the yogurt flavor and topping. The counter draws a curved line that emphasizes the customers' smooth movement through the shop.

There are pop signs that show the customers how to make the frozen yogurt (washing hands, dishing yogurt, and choosing the topping). These make the experience enjoyable and fun.

01-02. Interior overview
03. Topping counter
04. Eat-in space

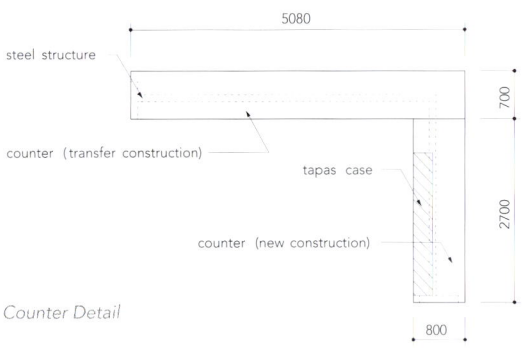

Counter Detail

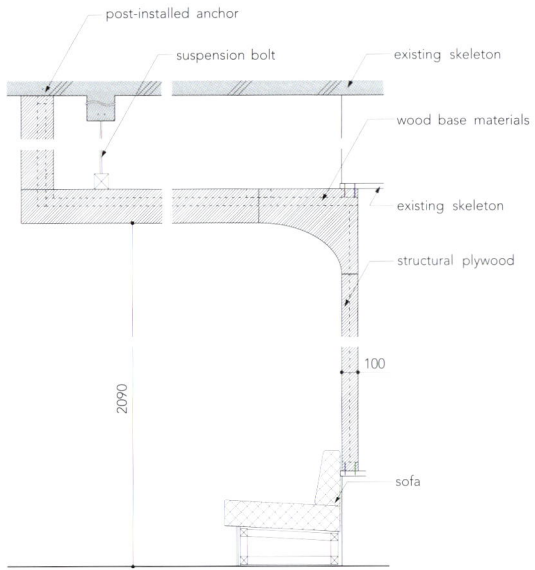

Louver Detail

Chowa

DESIGNER SALHAUS **USE** Restaurant **LOCATION** Yokohama, Japan **AREA** 94.63m²
PHOTOGRAPHER Toshiyuki Yano

Chowa is a bar & dining room located along Yokohama's Isezaki Shopping Street, known for the live performances by street musicians. Performances of various genres such as pop and jazz take place during weekends, making the shopping street a unique place.

Two key design concepts characterize this bar. Firstly, it is a place where one can dine and listen to live music. We wanted the bar to be a hangout for people gathering for the various street music and indoor music performances. In order to create a better acoustic environment for live music performances, the bar's interior surfaces are covered predominantly with timber-based materials. The regular, rib-like array of plywood and expanded aluminum sheets in between, covering the wall and ceiling, enhance the room acoustics, as well as creating a cozy ambience as if being surrounded by trees.

Secondly, we wanted to make conversation between bar staff and customers easier, especially around the bar counter. The bar counter is made of solid bubinga, and the levels of floor, bar counter and seats are determined so that the standing bar staff and seated customers can make eye contact easily. The bar counter brings people together, and provides a great place to enjoy a conversation.

01. Interior detail
02. Facade
03-04. Interior overview

03

04

05-07. Interior details

① Logo Screen
② Acoustic Aluminum Expanded Metal Lath
③ Display
④ Storage
⑤ WC
⑥ Counter
⑦ Kitchen
⑧ Anteroom

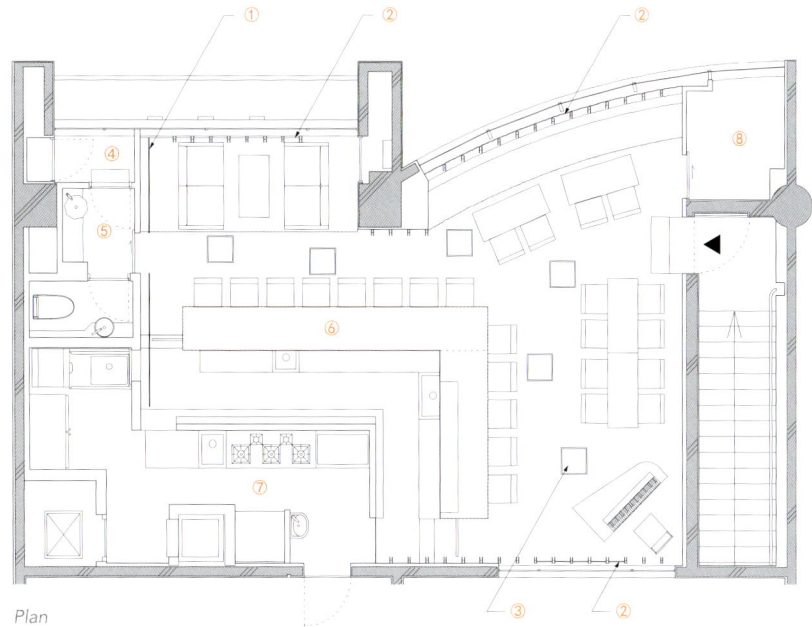

Plan

09-11. Interior overview

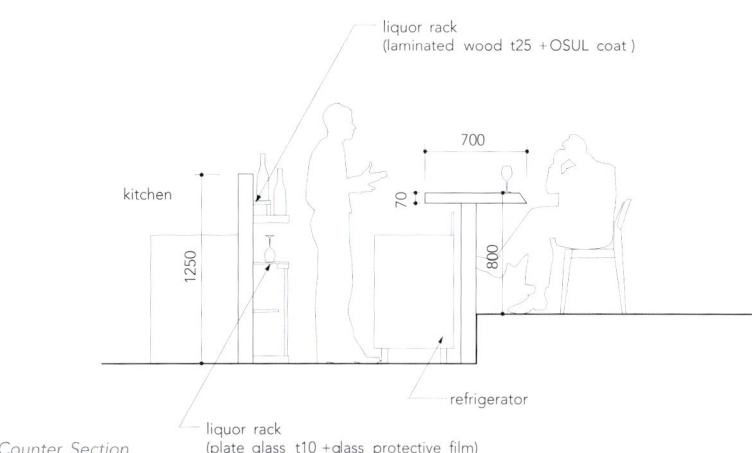

Counter Section

10

11

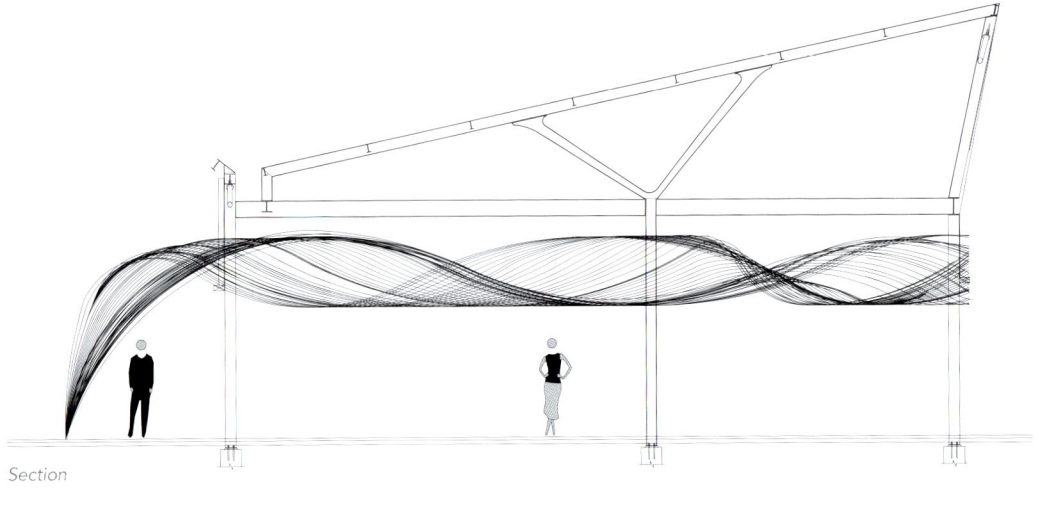

Section

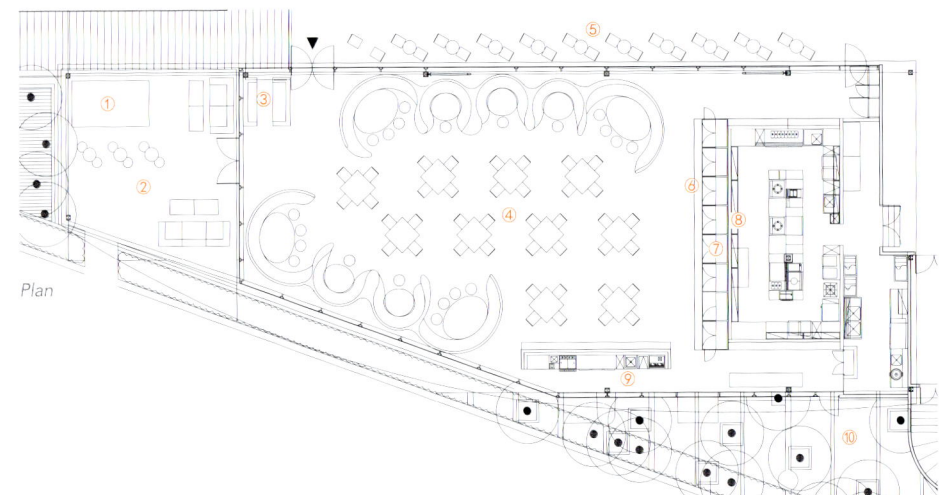

Plan

① Mobile Bar
② Outside Seating
③ Reception Cashier
④ Seating
⑤ Corridor
⑥ Wine Display
⑦ Wine Cooler
⑧ Show Kitchen
⑨ Bar
⑩ Outdoor Garden

Teeq

DESIGNER Yuhkichi Kawai / design spirits co., ltd.　**USE** Restaurant　**LOCATION** Kuala Lumpur, Malaysia　**CLIENT** YTL Land Sdn. Bhd.　**AREA** 555m²　**PHOTOGRAPHER** Zainudin Ashard

This restaurant, Teeq, was planned in Kuala Lumpur Malaysia, on the 8th floor roof parking space of the existing shopping center named as lot 10 which greets the 20th anniversary. I felt fortunate as I was able to participate and design for the master plan which included a club, theater, restaurant and the place of the courtyard.

I chose the location to match with the scenery even that would not be the great scenery for the view. Based on that, I concentrated more on the ceiling design because that was the only part that not surrounded by the restaurant with the glass keeping scenery.

Nevertheless, the ceiling design that I aimed was praised by lot of visitors where being without either disturbance, beautiful or too showy. However, the execution was repeated from trial due to various errors occurred as I wanted to make it an impressive entrance welcomes guests to an avant-garde decoration with undulating waves of wooden ribs encircling the ceiling. I think it has taken me around 2 months for the trial manufacture. After all, I hung the strip of the wood board with wire directly and attached the LED to the board and irradiated LED take the base right.

MATERIALS
floor　Nyatoh timber 150mm width, clear urethane gloss finish (PU coating);
internal wall　glass (architect wall), mirror 6mmTHK, stainless steel mirror polish finish 2mmTHK, gypsum board 12mm THK, laminate board wood pattern;
ceiling layer 1　gypsum board 12mmTHK painted light beige, printed sticker same pattern as Nyatoh 50mm width;
ceiling layer 2　steel plate 50mm width 1mmTHK, Nyatoh plywood veneer 50mm width, hung from gypsum board ceiling by fishing line

AWARDS
Best 100 of JCD, Japanese Commercial Environment Designers Association
Nomination Award of the Asia Pacific Interiors Design Biennial Awards, Shanghai Industry Design Association
Nomination Award of Display Design Award, Japan Display Design Association
Honorary Mention Award of International Design Awards, USA

01-02. Interior overview

03. Ceiling
04-05. Interior details

04

05

221

Aluminum Flower Garden

DESIGNER Moriyuki Ochiai Architects **USE** Restaurant / Bar, Event Space **AREA** 80m² **CLIENT** ronwit **CONSTRUCTOR** Aslego **PHOTOGRAPHER** Tetsu Hiraga

During the course of planning the layout for the Aluminum Flower Garden restaurant / bar and event space, we were challenged to come up with a concept that would evoke the floral imagery of the establishment's eponymous name.
In a country with limited resources such as Japan, the spirit of Monodzukuri is the epitome of ingenuity at the service of craftsmanship.
From a single sheet of paper, which can be folded into a variety of shapes, emerged the art of Origami.
From a single bolt of fabric was born one of Japan's most iconic garments: the Kimono.
From a single piece of cloth, which can be used to wrap and carry all sorts of objects, came the Furoshiki.
Taking inspiration from this cultural background, we used a single finite material, aluminum, as a simple planar surface from which we created an engaging three-dimensional space that fulfills various functions and requirements at once.
A sheet of aluminum, a recyclable material as thin and flexible as paper, spreads across the ceiling as it fills the space with its light and airy presence.
The creases in the aluminum are as many glittering and fluttering petals covering the ceiling and enfolding visitors in a flowery embrace.
Changes to the size and density of the flower petals impart the function and atmosphere suited to each area, such as lively and quiet areas created through minute differences in the height and expanse of a given space.
One's position and angle of vision as well as the reflection of images and lights from the mirrors on the walls concur to perpetually redefine the appearance of the whole space, thus enabling the viewer to experience a space with transient and diverse atmospheres.
The layering of minutely differing areas throughout the space gives people the opportunity to find an oasis of comfort at their own leisure.
As flowers bloom in all their glory, this delicate yet splendid

01. Full view (mirror)
02. Detail
03-04. Full view

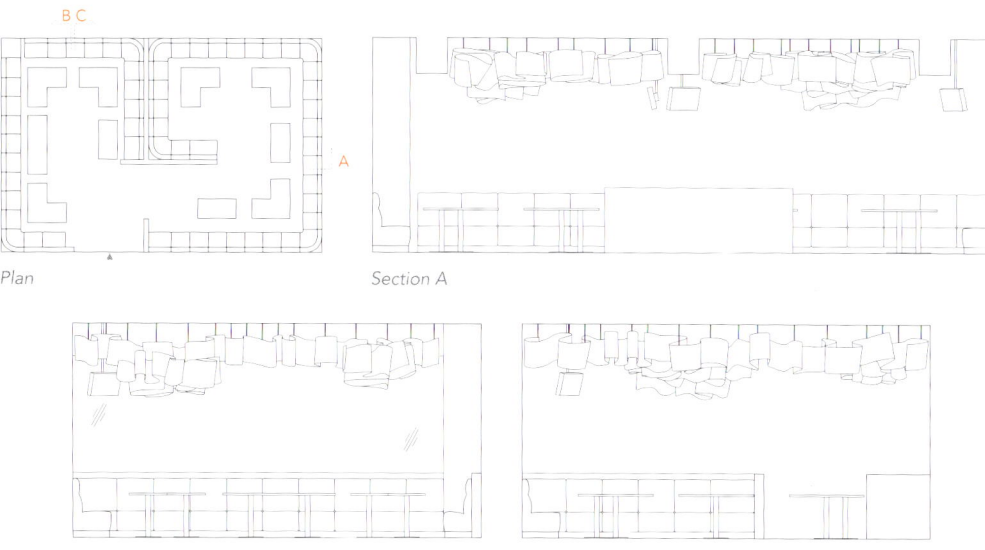

Plan *Section A*

Section B *Section C*

flower garden provides everyone with moments of delight. Moreover, since they give the space its singularity, we adopted the assembly method of the aluminum ceiling parts so as to be able to disassemble and reinstall them when moving the business to a different location. By doing so, we devised a way to effectively reduce the costs of moving.

MATERIALS
ceiling *recycled aluminum sheet, skeleton AEP*
floor *stone tile*
wall *painted drywall*

01. Construction technique
02. Interior wall
03. Interior detail
04. Paper wall
05. Indoor activity

Sketches

Abenoma

DESIGNER Abenoma / Naoya Matsumoto Design / Play Ground **USE** Bar **LOCATION** Abenoku, Osaka, Japan **AREA** 21m² **PHOTOGRAPHER** Takeshi Asano, Shizuka Takahashi

This is the project that young designers meet and cooperate to make a place where people get together in Abeno (near Tennoji), Osaka. There used to be a row house at a back alley in a part of Abeno and now it has been remodeled into a gallery space called "Abenoma".
We produced a self-built space by using an uncommon but simple material "tracing paper" with local residents. I found it interesting because it is fun to crumple paper and anybody can do it. This huge space made by paper is like a secret base and turns into a bar at night. I hope people get together and make new friends there and enjoy the space. This is the project by folding, pasting, sticking paper to make a space and hopefully to stick people together, stick people and the space as well.

01. Outdoor
02. Overview
03. Interior

Cafe/Day

DESIGNER SUPPOSE DESIGN OFFICE Co., Ltd.   **USE** Cafe   **LOCATION** Numazu city, Shizuoka, Japan   **AREA** 73.71m²   **PHOTOGRAPHER** Toshiyuki Yano

When you give a name to an object it inherits the function of the name but if you design a place without a name then it is free to develop its own name by the occurring activities. Cafe/day is located within a quiet residential area 5 minutes from the train station of Numazu-shi, Shizuoka. The project was to renovate two units of an "Izakaya" (Japanese style bar) located on a ground floor of a two story building.

In front of the building there are car parks, a road, and a driving school and it feels like the road continued forever. When you observe the driving school, there were a lot of yellow cars and even the poles that configured the driving lane were yellow. The color yellow was very influential and the surrounding feature gave influence in designing the cafe.

The plan was to make the two Izakaya into one big space by demolishing the party wall and to selectively demolish parts of the wall to open up the space. The counter, lighting fixtures, and fixed furniture were painted to a single color to make it abstract and erase the name of Izakaya from the space. The only new material that was used was the flooring, the most apparent feature of the surrounding; asphalt was continued into the shop and identifies the internal space and external space by the white lines on the floor. The cafe was able to establish itself as a true open cafe.

The furniture also incorporates the characteristic of the outdoor space. The bench was designed to mimic a bus stop bench and for the sofa, the car seats were modified and changed to become a sofa. Inside the cafe, similar to the driving school, the color yellow have been placed in the cafe and it creates a feel that the cafe is a part of the driving school. We designed the space so that the bar counter to became book shelves, and the Izakaya itself to a cafe and the activities of gathering, talking and drinking coffee made the it more like a cafe.

We used power of names in a paradoxical manner and found a new approach a design process in renovation works. We would like to start with no names in the process of designing in future.

04-07 Details

Plan

① Stroage
② Kitchen
③ WC

Saboten, Hong Kong

DESIGNER 4N Architects   **USE** Restaurant   **LOCATION** Hong Kong, China   **PHOTOS** 4N Architects

Saboten restaurant brings back the architectural interests of Shinjuku Japan with an innovative relationship between soft texture and rigid space. The design conveys a sense of purity and integrity of principle design elements, and epitomizes the sophistication of traditional Japanese architecture. It's even so slightly exotic and mysterious, yet comforting at the same time.

There is a very clear relationship between rich texture and space. We draw on the red and timber color served as key elements in design, decorated with the Nautical-style rope curtains that hang from ceiling to floor adding a touch of contemporary elegance. Upon arriving at the ground floor lobby, guests are welcomed by vermilion rope curtains floating along the stairs and cylindrical light boxes. We also used timber in order to emphasize with the continuity of the ceiling panels though the window seat to outside decor, clients may sit back and relax on the earth-tone sofa and booth seats while overlooking the dynamic city life through glass windows. The seating is carefully divided in a rigid manner, and the Quatrefoil mahogany style pattern signifies the sparkling and moves forward progressively.

The interior reflects a modern aesthetic, while still embracing a sense of comfort that mimics the food it serves. Each Tonkatsu makes your order come in a set, which means you also get an appetizer, miso soup, rice and of course a copious amount of shredded cabbage—all of which is refillable to your heart's desire.

Hailing from Shinjuku, Tokyo, Saboten first opened its doors in 1966 with the goal of serving the best Tonkatsu and now it has flourished into one of the largest chains moving forward progressively in Hong Kong. Cactus, the symbol of the brand is showcased at the shop entrance as a reminder while the decorative potted plants awake a sense of nature. History of Saboten vibrating by photos through the years displayed of the pillar along the side of the stairs to the top. The main dining hall, which accommodates 84 diners, boasts a warm color palette and booth seating, while luminous brand logos create a lively contrast.

01. A sense of touch
02. The staircase with rope curtains decoration
03. Interior detail
04. The brand's symbol, the cactus showcased at the shop entrance
05. Booth seats divided in rigid manner with Quatrefoil mahogany style pattern decoration on the glass

06. Purity and integrity of principle design elements
07. Quatrefoil mahogany style pattern
08. The design used timber in order to emphasize the continuity of the ceiling panels though the window seat to outside décoration

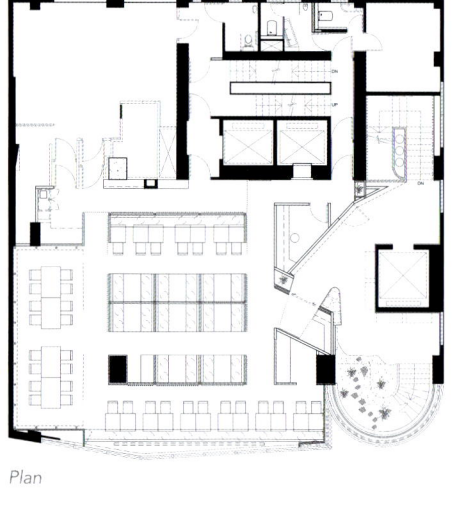

Plan

09-12. Feature room
13. Rope curtains with custom made chair and LED lighting

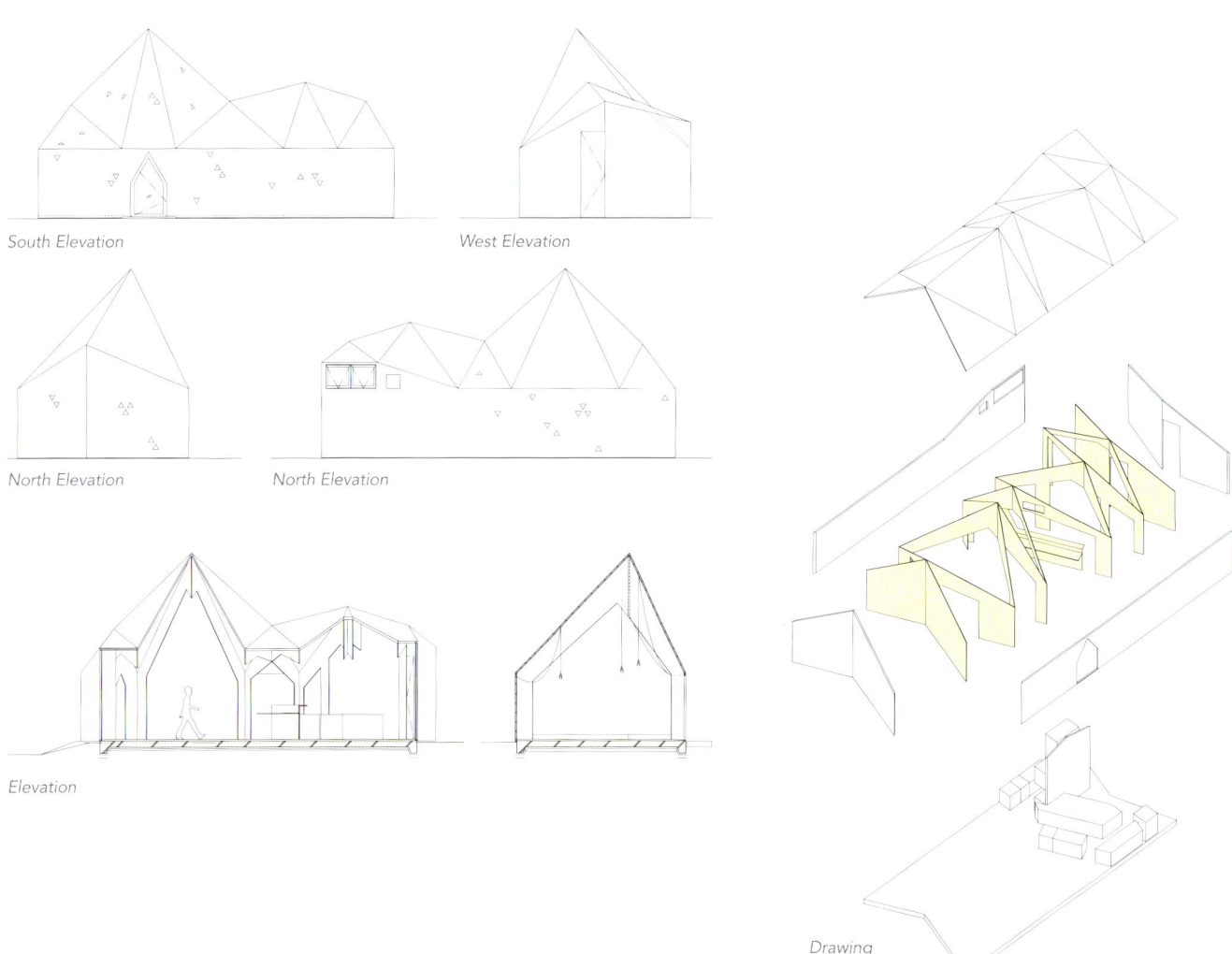

South Elevation *West Elevation*

North Elevation *North Elevation*

Elevation

Drawing

L'angolino

DESIGNER GENETO   **USE** Restaurant   **LOCATION** Gunma, Japan   **AREA** 60.95m²
PHOTOGRAPHER Yasutake Kondo

This is an Italian restaurant in Gunma prefecture. In contrast to a big city, this town has a typical local city view. There are many chain stores and giant shopping stores on the roadside. When the client originally came here he had a strong thought that his hometown should have identity and it needs a place (restaurant) which can be a foothold for local people. We researched the building forms and the use in this town. We tried to get identity as a restaurant and make an opportunity to change the town by making a building form not existing here. The client thought that the building has a statement toward the town and it arises from the construction stage already. He decided to build as self-build and had a communication actively for the locals passing by during the construction.

On the premise of the self-build and the building form not existing here, we conceived the simple structure by plywood. The building form became the pointed roof shape not existing in this town. It's monocoque construction consisting of the structural plywood portal frame (t=24mm) and the exterior wall (t=59mm).

The exterior is covered with FRP waterproof. The thin exterior wall carries the atmosphere of the inside to outside with light, sound and smell. Avoiding to be connecting the inside and the outside directly, the small triangle windows are built. In inside, the space is separating gently by the portal frame crossing in a net-like. The kitchen and the hall are same room to bring a live aspect between chef and customer. The structure is the result of looked for the limit of skills by self-build, and the building facade is creating a totally different view in the town. We expect it will develop the identity as a landmark by that the locals get together.

MATERIALS
structural plywood, FRP

01-02. Facade
03-04. Interior overview

① Kitchen
② Hall
③ Toilet

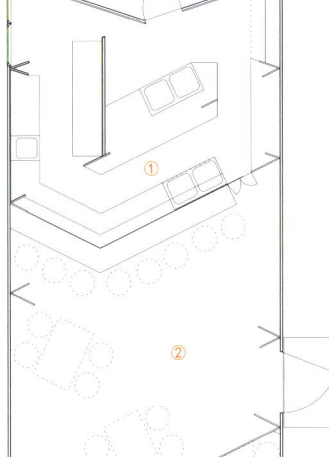

Plan

05-07. Interior details

01. Temporary construction as a bar
02. Texture
03. Activity inside the bar

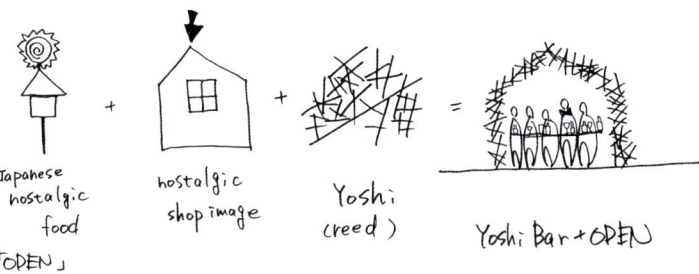

Sketch

Yoshi Bar 2nd

DESIGNER Naoya Matsumoto, Seian University of Arts and Design Students   **USE** Bar   **LOCATION** Otsu City, Shiga, Japan   **PHOTOGRAPHER** Takeshi Asano

This is the second time I used reed, which is grown in Biwako, Shiga, as a material for a stall for college festival. For the last time I used it simply for a place to sell Oden, one of the Japanese traditional food, this time I added the idea of "systematic".

First of all, I prepared six panels of reeds and put them (the front, back, left, right and the tops for the roof parts) together with reeds. As a panel it doesn't stand itself yet but putting them together and building them makes it possible to stand and gives us some space inside. Seen from the front of the stall structured randomly but systematically, the stall looks like a gabled roof which is familiar to the Japanese. Oden, also is familiar and usually reminds us of our mom's cooking. A small discovery of a roof and a memory of their mom's cooking made the people relaxed and buy food with a warm feeling in a chilly day.

It takes only a couple of days to build this type of stall and it can be built easily. I would like to have more opportunities to provide some spaces like this kind of temporary stall for the future project.

① Locker Room
② Semi Private Dining
③ Dish Wash
④ Walk in Chiller
⑤ Beverage Stock
⑥ Ice Bed
⑦ Dry Stock

Nautilus

DESIGNER Yuhkichi Kawai / design spirits co.,ltd **USE** Restaurant **LOCATION** Singapore **CLIENT** AC2 International Pte. Ltd. **PHOTOGRAPHER** Toshihide Kajiwara

The Nautilus Project is located on the fourth floor of the ION shopping center, opened recently on the Orchard Road, Singapore. The great strategy of the location has brought lot of benefits to the floor composite of sales, drinks and food. Besides, the entrance of the restaurant is flanked on one side by an oyster bar and on the other side by displays of delectable dessert and trays of fresh crustaceans on ice.
A certain concept of the interior design, chef and location have been arranged by the food consultant from the beginning, which has caused my difficulty in directing for our targeted interior design. However, the owner is the president of the cargo company and her beauty made me decided to reflect her sophisticate, elegant and tender characteristics to this restaurant project.
It was a challenge to make the entrance which opens to mall's passageway for guests to access easily without any hesitation. Curve walls at the entrance lead the guests to enter the restaurant naturally, and the opening kitchen adds interactive experiences as well.

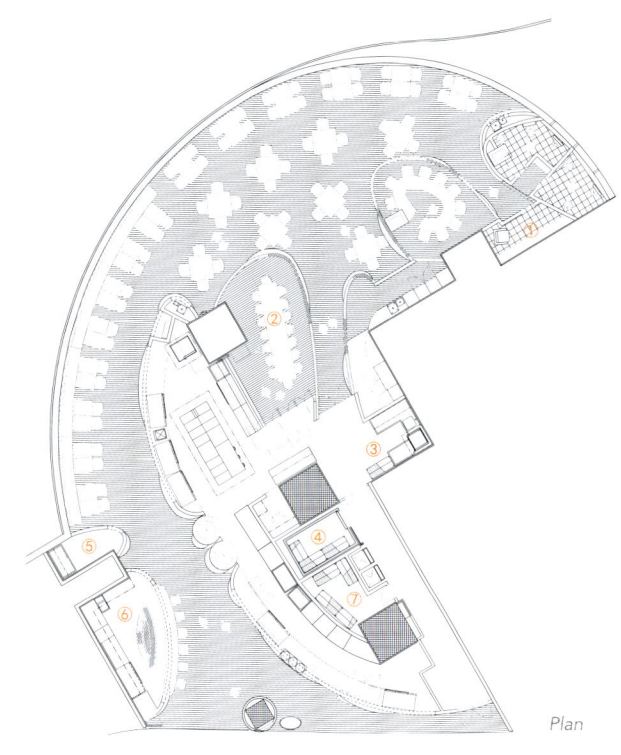

Plan

01. Entrance
02-03. Interior overview

04. Seating area
05-08. Interior details

245

Tokyo Kushi Bar

DESIGNER Akitoshi Imafuku / supermaniac Inc.　**USE** Standing bar　**LOCATION** Tokyo, Japan
AREA 18.56cm²　**PHOTOGRAPHER** Nacasa & Partners Inc

"A creative design to renew the idea of standing bars in Japan", we hold it for the slogan of the project, the design that is one of a kind. The 7 pillars connecting the counter top to the suspended ceiling are made of a solid surface: Corian. The Corian is thermoformed by skilled craftsmen, and it is a rare example in the world of transforming Corian into such curvilinear form. By putting LED lights in those pillars on the top and the bottom, we designed the bar wrapped with soft lights. Only several down lights are placed in the kitchen area. The curvilinear forms of the counter and the suspending ceiling are inspired by the beautiful clouds people see from the small airplane window, and the lighting pillars are also the image of the sunbeams streaming through the clouds. In this way, we transformed the users' image of standing bars, which in turn improves the quality of standing bars.

01. Interior overview
02. Facade
03-04. Interior details

① WC
② Kitchen
③ CT

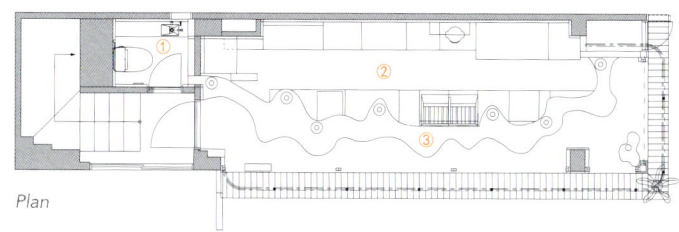

Plan

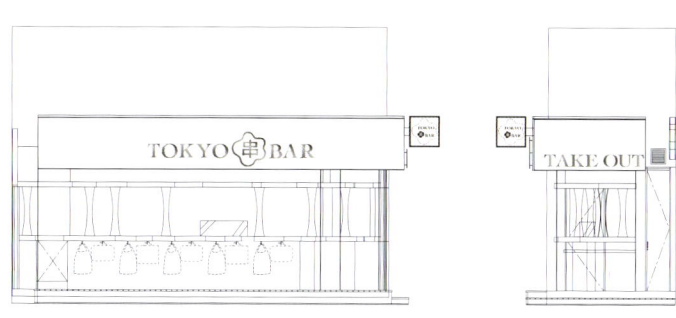

Elevation

Sushi Tsujita

DESIGNER Takeshi Sano / SWeeT co.,ltd. **USE** Restaurant **LOCATION** Los Angeles, USA **AREA** 137.16m² **PHOTOGRAPHER** Nacasa & Partners Inc.

This Tsujita Group's project is the 3rd project in L.A. and the restaurant specializes in sushi. The building is located behind the patio, so there should be something that attracts people from the street or even people in the car, especially those in the automobile society L.A. The gorgeous chandelier, which is located at patio, works as an eye-catcher to notify the existence of the restaurant.

Sushi Tsujita has the finest quality sushi, and constantly changes their taste by the seasonal food, is served by a professional Edomae-style sushi chef. I expressed the consistent change by demonstrating the idea of kaleidoscope using hexagonal bamboo panels. The bamboo panels, which are arranged geometrically and randomly, will consistently change their appearances, which depends on where people stand. The effect makes people feel as if they are in the world of kaleidoscope.

In addition, bamboo keeps the interior clean because of its bactericidal effect. And also its healing effect makes people relaxed, therefore people can focus on their dishes and their taste. I hope that the delicious food and the artistic interior provided by Sushi Tsujita will grow and flourish strongly in L.A. like bamboo does.

MATERIALS
bamboo, mirror

01. Interior overview
02. Entrance
03-05. Interior details

06. Booth Area
07. Entry

① Entry
② Terrace
③ Sofa Area
④ Booth Area
⑤ Counter Area
⑥ Kitchen
⑦ WC

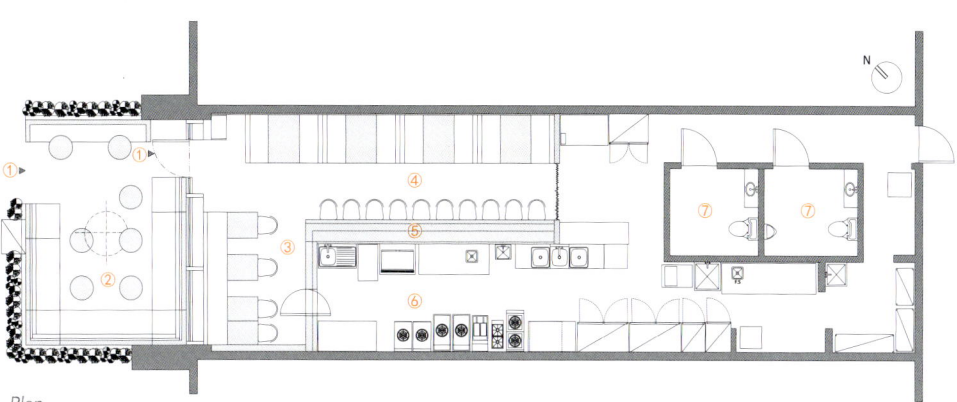

Plan

08-10. Seating area
11. Interior wall feature

INDEX

P230-235 **4N Architects**
www.4narchitects.com

P120-125 **Adrià Goula**
www.adriagoula.com

P200-203 **andfujiizaki**
andfujiizaki.jp

P126-129 **Asylum**
theasylum.com.sg

P42-47, P54-59 **CASE-REAL**
www.casereal.com

P48-53 **Claesson Koivisto Rune Architects**
www.claessonkoivistorune.se

P64-67 **Curiosity Design**
curiosity.jp

P20-25 **CUT architectures**
www.cut-architectures.com

P80-85 **designground55**
dground55.com

P168-171 **design office Dress Inc.**
d-dress.net

P218-221, P242-245 **design spirits co. , ltd**
www.design-spirits.com

P98-101 **DESIGN STUDIO CROW**
www.studio-crow.jp

P150-155, P172-175 **DOYLE COLLECTION co. ltd.**
www.doylecollection.jp

P120-125 **EL EQUIPO CREATIVO**
en.elequipocreativo.com

P208-209	**emmanuelle moureaux**	
	www.emmanuelle.jp	

| P136-139 | **Facet Studio** |
| | www.facetstudio.com.au |

| P236-239 | **GENETO** |
| | www.geneto.net |

| P110-115 | **Golucci International Design** |
| | www.golucci.com |

| P94-97 | **HaKo Design** |
| | www.hakodesign.com |

| P116-119 | **Hiroyuki Ogawa Architects Inc.** |
| | www.ogawaoffice.com |

| P196-199 | **id inc.** |
| | www.id-inc.jp |

| P140-143 | **Jean de Lessard** |
| | delessard.com |

| P16-19, P90-93, P106-109 | **Kengo Kuma & Associates** |
| | kkaa.co.jp |

| P130-135 | **k-studio** |
| | www.k-studio.gr |

| P72-75 | **MOMENT** |
| | www.momentdesign.com |

| P38-41, P222-223 | **Moriyuki Ochiai Architects** |
| | www.moriyukiochiai.com |

| P64-67 | **Nacasa & Partners Inc.** |
| | www.nacasa.co.jp |

| P60-63, P190-195, P224-225, P240-241 | **Naoya Matsumoto Design** |
| | www.naoyamatsumoto.com |

| P182-185 | **nendo** |
| | www.nendo.jp |

| P34-37 | **Niji Architects** |
| | www.niji-architects.com |

P156-161 **PRISM DESIGN**
prism_design.prosite.com

P204-207 **PROCESS5 DESIGN Co., Ltd.**
process5.com

P212-217 **SALHAUS**
salhaus.com

P176-181 **sinato**
www.sinato.jp

P6-9 **STILE**
www.go-go-stile.com

P30-33 **Studio Arihiro Miyake**
theasylum.com.sg

P246-247 **supermaniac Inc.**
www.supermaniac.ne.jp

P186-189 **Super Potato**
www.superpotato.com

P226-229 **SUPPOSE DESIGN OFFICE Co., Ltd.**
www.suppose.jp

P248-253 **SWeeT co.,ltd.**
www.sweetdesign.jp

P68-71, P86-89, P102-105 **Tetsuya Matsumoto**
www.matsuya-art-works.co.jp

P26-29 **TORAFU ARCHITECTS**
torafu.com

P144-149, P162-167 **Vie Studio**
www.viestudio.com.au

P76-79 **Yamazaki Kentaro Design Workshop**
ykdw.org

P210-211 **Yasuhiro Sone**
sonedesign.co.jp

P10-15 **Yuko Nagayama & Associates**
www.yukonagayama.co.jp